Marbles on the Floor

Akron Series in Contemporary Poetics

Akron Series in Contemporary Poetics
Mary Biddinger and John Gallaher, Editors
Nick Sturm, Associate Editor
Jordan McNeil, Associate Editor

Marbles on the Floor

How to Assemble a Book of Poems

Sarah Giragosian & Virginia Konchan, eds.

The University of Akron Press
Akron, Ohio

ISBN: 978-1-62922-254-7 (paper)
ISBN: 978-1-62922-255-4 (ePDF)
ISBN: 978-1-62922-256-1 (ePub)

A catalog record for this title is available from the Library of Congress.

The paper used in this publication meets the minimum requirements of ANSI NISO z 39.48–1992 (Permanence of Paper). ∞

Cover: Photo by JJ Ying on Unsplash. Cover design by Amy Freels.

Marbles on the Floor was designed and typeset in Garamond with Alegreya Sans titles by Amy Freels and printed on sixty-pound natural and bound by Baker & Taylor Publisher Services of Ashland, Ohio.

"Of Bonsais and Moons: An Epistolary on Making a Book of Poems" is copyright © Victoria Chang.

"Restless Herd: Some Thoughts on Order—in Poetry, in Life" was first published by *Poets & Writers Magazine* (May/June 2021). Reprinted by permission of the publisher, Poets & Writers, Inc., 90 Broad Street, New York, NY 10004. www.pw.org.

Affordable Learning Initiative
THE UNIVERSITY OF AKRON

Produced in conjunction with the University of Akron Affordable Learning Initiative. More information is available at www.uakron.edu/affordablelearning/

For Marvin Campbell, in memory
Poet, Scholar, Friend

Contents

Introduction

STYLE IN WRITING is hard to pin down. Like any poetry that feels vital, that revels in paradox and mystery, style feels to the reader both inevitable and surprising. When it comes to poetry, one's signature style (manifest through tone and other literary elements) is also somewhat mysterious—we often can't put a finger on what instantly reveals the author of this or that poem.

A signature style—and by this, we also mean creating a dreamscape, dramatic tension, narrative, argument, dialectic, and arc—once found or achieved, however, makes everything about writing, editing, and publishing easier, including the Herculean feat of assembling a poetry manuscript for publication, a task rendered more difficult and opaque for the relative paucity of craft texts on the subject.

Just as there is no ready-made compositional formula, heuristic, syllogism, or algorithm for poetry or its reception by a reader or reading public, there is also no one, true, proven, repeatable, or even identifiable way to assemble a book of poems. Most poets can relate to the Stevensian "rage for order," but too often, the unnecessary shrouding of mystification surrounding poetry and the poetic process, or accusations of obscurantism, elitism, or irrelevance keep poets from openly discussing the art and science behind the actual material construction of a book. We found that the craft of manuscript assembly was little discussed in craft texts or poetry forums, with a few notable exceptions, including Jeffrey Levine's blog, April Ossmann's article "Thinking Like an Editor: How to Order Your Poetry Manuscript," and the anthology *Ordering the Storm: How to Put Together a Book of Poems* (2006), edited by Susan Grimm.

Seeking to open up the conversation, *Marbles on the Floor: How to Assemble a Book of Poems* was conceived from a poetic dialogue on how to shed light on this process through the articulated experiential wisdom of poets in all stages of their careers. What follows, then, is an anthology of interconnected essays (craft, lyric, and critical) on the art and technique of poetry manuscript assembly. With this timely, invaluable, and compact resource for creative writing teachers, as well as emerging and established poets honing their craft, writers in other genres (fiction and non-) will also benefit from this widely applicable yet nuanced discussion of how to bring a book into being.

The anthology is no easier to summarize or categorize than the genre of poetry itself: our eclectic contingent of poet-contributors deploy lyric, scholarly, teacherly, documentary, autobiographical, and epistolary modes to address the subject, exploring everything from how arranging a manuscript facilitated the evolution of their own poetic consciousnesses to how to identify an organizing structural principle in one's work: a prevailing shape, form, or concept. Discursively, others coined or identified sets of terms: collocative and generative, intuition and logic, Apollonian and Dionysian; included close readings of contemporary poetry collections; invoked the materiality and tangibility of the manuscript and archive; engaged with literary history and the visual arts; and created ingenious framing conceits for their essays, such as bookshelf assembly instructions and a FAQ. Levity abounds (three poets mention throwing a manuscript down the stairs as a chance-based procedure), and while wildly diverse in conception, style, and approach, all twelve poets emphasized, in turns, both the idiosyncratic as well as context-specific process of constructing a poetry manuscript, as an individualized gestalt that is more than, yet inextricable from, the sum of its parts.

Twenty-first-century poetry in the US is as diverse as its practitioners, offering novel modes and contexts that require new forms of theorizing, particularly of craft practices. How do we begin to conceptualize the sequencing of the poetry manuscript, with its exhilarating valences and aesthetic challenges, and how do we interpret the complex ecosystem of the poetry collection? What are the initiating impulses that shape a poet's thoughts about order and how do we make a relatively intuitive process legible for others? How might we nurture the stamina and flexibility of thought that manuscript assembly demands? All of these questions, among others, were the genesis for this anthology, which entwines practical advice with lyric musings that chart the aesthetic and meaning-making possibilities involved in the assembly of the poetry manuscript.

Opening the anthology with humor and lyrical aplomb, Diane Seuss's "Restless Herd" wends its way through the switchbacks of autobiography, poetic legacy, tropes of binding and identity-making, unbinding and reckoning with the self's otherness, as well as poetic theory, all the while suggesting that the processes of realizing the poetry collection and actualizing the self-as-poet occur in tandem. Both entail a kind of reckoning with one's emotional life, giving shape to a mythopoetics and to a narrative arc or thesis: "Maybe the binding, the thesis, the order all shore us up against death. At least as a container for death. Maybe unbinding is to open our arms to death (and grief and Eros and hallucination), to forces that can't be compressed, denied, or contained. To chaos. To the guidance of the dead." Emily Dickinson is at once mother, talisman, and tour guide through the chapter, as Seuss retraces her encounters with facsimiles of Dickinson's constructed herbarium, which also inflect scholars' contemplative processes of arrangement rearrangement that have been taken with her fascicles throughout history. Seuss invites readers to take seriously the proposition "that order is a birthright, as is disorder," asking us to trust in the inevitable pleating of intuition and craft when we stitch, unstitch, and re-stitch our own poems into order. The classificatory and the imaginative impulses in making a book are not binary proclivities, she reminds us, but in a rich conversation with one another.

Next, Heather Treseler's chapter "Poems as Paintings: Life-Drawing in Words" showcases the poet-critic's metaphorical imagination, her inquiry into the relation between poetry and visual art, and poetry's communal ethos—the channeling of other voices and mentors who are filtered through the poetic consciousness or—as Treseler writes—"We are radios of alternating frequencies, traveling in and out of reception zones; we are galleries of tableaux we have not ourselves made. This is the largesse of art, which spares us the isolating bewilderment of raw experience." She theorizes the implications for the poet-reader who might be interested in negotiating the critical and interpretive process of ekphrastic writing with interiorization and lyrical experiment. Her essay also explores the burgeoning of the poetic consciousness, as it opens with a scene in which the poet-to-be first experiences the visceral impact of metaphor. Relaying her poetic origins slantwise, she marks her father's valediction as the inception of poetic consciousness, the "trapdoor metaphor" opening up the junctural possibilities of poetic time and the metaphysics of metaphor. Questions of manuscript order entail a sensory provocation ("a splinter in the senses"), an engagement with a sympathetic reader, and museum curation. Trafficking in metaphor, Treseler's chapter weaves together the personal, curatorial, collaborative, teacherly, and ekphrastic preoccupations of her own chapbook *Parturition*.

Another teacherly chapter, "FAQ: from Press Authors, Graduate Students, and Editing Clients" by Christopher Salerno, uses a "Frequently Asked Questions" form as a model for a Socratic editorial dialogue between himself and the poets he's worked with over the years, offering thorough, near-exhaustive answers to thirteen salient questions of manuscript assembly on topics ranging from narrative chronology, order, "aboutness," theme and project books, sectioning, juxtapositions between poems and across the book, the prepublication of poems, and knowing when dozens of poems constitute a book. Attentive to the human and cultural predilection for a narrative arc ("We have Freytag's dramatic 'Pyramid' tattooed on our bones"), Salerno's clever essay, steeped in editorial savoir faire, abounds with helpful exercises for poets working on manuscripts, such as "Try reading the catalogue copy for your favorite poetry distributor, and then see whether you can write a three-hundred-word description of your own book," and virtuosically answers, with an insider's knowledge, questions many poets may have oft-pondered alone, or have never thought to ask, when constructing (and at times deconstructing) the "dynamic architecture" of a book.

The reader will find more practical exercises in Annie Finch's ground-breaking essay "The Body of the Poetry Manuscript: Patterning Your Collection with Structural Repetition." Why should free verse be equated with structural absence or organizational chaos? Finch establishes structural repetition as the single defining characteristic of poetry, then champions for a poet's establishment of a capacious yet unifying "organizing structural principle" (OSP) in their books, one which operates on multiple levels, including syllable count, word-music, phrase, syntax, stanzas, form, and the level of the book itself. Finch likens the manuscript to a living, branching tree to consider the hypotactic structure in a book of poems: "If the whole book is like the trunk, and the individual poems are like leaves, then the sections that keep everything unified and vibrant are like the branches of the tree." Ultimately, Finch provides a three-step process for identifying structural patterns, a guide to the book revision process in light of these higher-level organizing elements, and a final set of practices from *A Poet's Craft: A Comprehensive Guide to Making and Sharing Your Poetry*, while emphasizing, in conjunction with other essays in the anthology, the power of one's poetic sensibility to arrange disparate poems together with attention to structural repetition. In the end, a book "interwoven through an OSP is more likely to be felt as a conversation," she says, and "the sublime, universal creative process underlying this organizational matrix—a web of connections inviting patterns of love and meaning, both within the book and between book and reader—is the discovery and nurturing of pattern."

Extending the inquiry into formal approaches to manuscript assembly, Stephen Kampa's "The Shapes of Books" takes as its premise a neologistic set of terms, collocative ("gathered and arranged") and generative ("conceived as a whole") books, then proceeds to investigate these terms, adding meaningful nuances as the essay accrues (collocative: arrangement, generative: contents). Offering compelling close readings—with meticulous attention to prosody—of Rachel Hadas, Ilya Kaminsky, Erica Dawson, and A. E. Stallings, Kampa doesn't argue for either animating premise, per se, instead exploring the strengths and risks inherent to each, and the intersections between them, across a poet's oeuvre: "The point of thinking about books as leaning toward the collocative or the generative, and to consider what coherence this affords them, is (again) not to advocate for a particular model, but rather to articulate options." Kampa's in-depth "case studies and conclusions," shaped around these fluid oppositions, and discussion of the controversial "project book" capture a moment in our literary zeitgeist, and also echo a prevailing theme of the anthology: "however many models you have at hand, and however much friendly help or editorial advice you get, only you can write your book."

Furthering the intrigue of manuscript order, Alyse Knorr's essay "Writing on the Wall: A Mystery" explores the enigma of manuscript manifestation through various analogies including the culinary arts, striking at the anthology's very ethos: "I think most poets do know what we're doing, but not always how or why we're doing it that way. Maybe if you read enough books of poetry, you internalize the 'feel' of a good order—a feeling described best not with logic but rather metaphor. The poet's native tongue." Fascinatingly, Knorr asks, in consideration of Ted Hughes's willed reassembly of Plath's *Ariel*, and the shocking difference between how she left the manuscript and how it was published: "How many different potential books are contained within the same stack of poems?" Likewise, how would one enact the philosophy of treating a book of poems as "one long poem"? Elliptical and evocative, Knorr's essay offers strategies for visual order mapping, creating syntactic, imagistic, and sonic closure, and moving between consciousnesses, including that of author and reader, and control and trust, at last embracing the mystery of the process.

Clarifying some of that mystery, "Some Assembly Required" by Harvey Hix takes as a structuring analogic principle the work of bookcase assembly: specifically, the set of instructions that are packed with the parts. Hix's practical, pedagogical, and workmanlike approach is something like the assembly instructions one dreams of receiving with a bookcase, but which rarely (depending on the manufacturer) arrive; his "Easy-to-Follow Step-by-Step Poetry Book Assembly Instructions" follow six clear steps, from selecting poems to checking one's work; optional instructions include getting physical and getting outside. All the instructions "invite repetition rather than precluding it," and can be conceived of in any order, but the main through line remains, that of parts/poems that are assembled into a whole, a book, and which, furthermore, are not intended to preclude, but rather to inform, one's own aesthetic judgment: "each resulting book unique, inimitable."

Does the thought of assembling a book of poems feel more like work than magic? Also absorbed by the materiality of the manuscript, Karyna McGlynn's essay "Leaping Between Seams: What Analog Collage Taught Me About Sequencing a Book of Poems," a deftly comedic, lyrical auto-biography, traces the poet's process of self-creation from her beginnings in Austin, Texas, where she haunted art supply stores as way of "vicariously absorbing the sort of credibility that still accompanies tangibility." Her discovery of surrealist collage allowed her to recapture the "psychedelic dream-logic of early childhood," and her essay artfully likens the work of collage to that of metaphor-making, and collage process videos to assembling a poetry manuscript, highlighting an undercurrent of the anthology, that one's personal aesthetic is the "glue that brings disparate pieces together." Asking "Why not show a tiger leaping from the mouth of a volcano? And why not replace the mouth of the volcano with the coral-lipsticked mouth of a screaming woman?," McGlynn draws a parallel between the poetic line and stanza and the juxtaposition and compression of collage as similar ways of controlling the flow of sensory data and embracing absurdity. Her essay concludes with a description of her process, akin to those advocated by other poets in the anthology, yet guided by a visual artist's imaginary, on the floor (gathering, grouping, letting "the seams speak to each other," and identifying keywords, such as prominent themes, topics, images, colors, locations, time periods, POVs, and formal attributes). McGlynn's delightful wit ("I'd spent half my life in workshops talking about the 'craft' of the 'trade' like some sort of medieval artisan's apprentice. At pubs across the Midwest, I'd gathered with fellow guildsmen!") echoes her "virtually identical" poetic impulse and collage aesthetic ("theatrical, female-centric, drag-influenced, darkly humorous & decidedly maximalist"), providing a perspective of wonder, play, and jouissance, one that advocates for interdisciplinarity and a return to the senses.

Next, Philip Metres's arresting chapter "Dreaming the Total Poem, Assembling the Counterarchive, Writing the Refuge" explores the palpable sense of literature as "country, a possible homeland" and maps his own corpus, which inflects documentary evidence, maps, images, music, juxtaposition, and palimpsests. Metres charts his political and personal forays into his poetry collections' meditations on cultural identity, war, historical memory, the politics of representation, and international conflict, such as the crisis between Palestine and Israel, as in his latest collection, *Shrapnel Maps*. Animated by a counterarchival impulse, a ballast against the nationalistic and mnemonic claims of hegemonic discourse, Metres's collection is invested in poetry's "parallel cultural labor of undoing erasure, of making visible and audible a history that the official narratives suppress or exclude." As he writes, "the counterarchive must see itself as something more fluid, more living, and less bound to documents—a laughing memory, a funeral dance, a mapped songline, worn prayer beads passed down. The counterarchive is not in a place, so a poetry book's relationship to that counterarchive will be like a thumbnail, jump drive, or hyperlink." In making decisions about order and arrangement that entail centering "other perspectives," Metres's chapter considers the temporal, geographical and dialogical organizational patterns that rupture monolithic nationalist narratives.

Also centering his reader's perspective in the art of manuscript assembly, Kazim Ali's epistolary address to the poet, "Dear Unexplainable," explores the architectural, geographic, personal and pedagogical valences of manuscript assembly. Perambulating through his own travels and education as a poet-critic, Ali provides an excursion into the architectonic and deconstructive dimensions of composing the serial poem and ordering the manuscript. After a stint in France where he experienced the challenge of second language acquisition and learned only "bits and scraps" of the French language, Ali abjured fluency in the name of "the beyond, the unknown, the startling, the misunderstood." Embracing cacophony and mystery, Ali considers the poem as a dynamic event, one that embraces and delights in discontinuity and fracture, while situating the reader as "the real creator of the book." Replete with agile turns and surprises, Ali's epistolary, labyrinthian chapter memorably charts the ways that the process of ordering the manuscript, "the wandering" becomes "the journey" itself.

Also invested in collections that interrogate a theme, Cyrus Cassells's chapter "Mystery and Legacy in Shaping a Manuscript" is a lyrical account of the mysteries of poetic consciousness and a testing of the tensile thread between mourning and celebration that galvanized his third book, *Beautiful Signor*. More specifically, the chapter explores the pivots between the book's wrestling with the griefwork of the AIDS crisis and a marshaling of joy and tenderness against an adversarial heteronormative imaginary. As a poet who works "almost exclusively in book-length cycles," Cassells explores the process of writing a gay text that is both a "recovery project" and in close alliance with "sonic beauty and indirection." As he indicates, writing a thematically connected poetry collection "often takes several years...which can be both frustrating and exhilarating in terms of the dogged detective work and ever-expanding odyssey required." In the case of *Beautiful Signor*, the odyssey took shape "out of outrage and politics. [Cassells] wrote it during the period of Senator Jesse Helms's ravings, amid a battery of poisonous public discourse about gay art and people." If gay desire exposes the fictions of self-possession and a stable and coherent identity, *Beautiful Signor* situates itself in the expressive and ontological hinterlands between protest and queer love, "outcry" and "joy."

Closing the anthology in a letter both elegiac and tender to her fellow poet-reader, Victoria Chang's chapter "Of Bonsais and Moons: An Epistolary on Making a Book of Poems" makes legible the process of listening and responding to the otherness of the poetry manuscript: "Similarly, your poems are from another you, from a moon that no longer exists. Each moon dies by morning.... Even so, each night, you still recognize the moon as a moon, despite never having met that particular moon before. This liminal space where the familiar and unfamiliar overlap is the space in which you will make a book of poems." Gesturing toward an enabling alterity, a generative site for re-seeing and reimagining one's poems, Chang both charts and enchants the practical and metaphorical striations in producing a book of poems. Caring for an ailing mother, for sensitive bonsai trees, for poems that are heirs of moons or—before they are collated together— "a stack of moons" that may or may not be the early semblance of a poetry collection: these images and tropes are concentric rings in Chang's chapter, which transposes the work of shaping a book to an ethics of care, and tending: "knowing that there is no one right way can be freeing. Each manuscript is like a different bonsai plant. Let the poems tell you what works for them, knowing each season may be different. Each time of day may bring about a different order, the rain or wind can affect order." Whatever the conditions of making, in the end, she writes, "so much about poetry is about faith."

Together, this collection's letters, essays, and experimental forms elucidate the often bewildering and slippery process of assembling a manuscript. This volume is not intended to be the final word on the process, but instead to carve open a space for continued dialogue about the craft of manuscript assembly. While the trajectory of the manuscript is ultimately up to the poet, this anthology can serve as a guide to the challenging yet rewarding process of ordering and sequencing. In doing so, the poet-reader may—like the poet-critics of the collection—come to better appreciate their own poetics and personal development as writers. What follows is an innovative craft guide, lyrical bildungsroman, and a nonprescriptive set of tools, by way of inspiring narratives, exercises, prompts, and other imaginative and concrete aides-mémoire.

In animating this esoteric and idiosyncratic process for readers and poets, we hope this anthology might enact the Dickinson poem that catalyzed the project, "I felt a Cleaving in my Mind," in reverse: "Sequence ravelling into Sound / Like Balls—upon a floor" (#937).

I felt a Cleaving in my Mind—
As if my Brain had split—
I tried to match it—Seam by Seam—
But could not make it fit.

The thought behind, I strove to join
Unto the thought before—
But Sequence ravelled out of Sound
Like Balls—upon a Floor.

—Emily Dickinson (#937)

Restless Herd

Some Thoughts on Order

Diane Seuss

I.

> *She had horses who danced in their mothers' arms. / She had horses who thought they were the sun and their / bodies shone and burned like stars. / She had horses who waltzed nightly on the moon. / She had horses who were much too shy, and kept quiet / in stalls of their own making.*
> —Joy Harjo, "She Had Some Horses"

WHEN I THINK of order, I think of horse statues.

As a child in rural Michigan, I coveted them. They could sometimes be found at Goodwill, and a couple of times, on a birthday, I received a new one from a family friend. I housed my collection on a special wooden shelf my dad built before he died. It sat on the floor. Low. Kid-level. Boarded there, they were objets d'art. Taken out to play, they became real, but more-than-real, expressions of the Platonic form of "horse." I brought them onto my bed and bent my right knee at an angle in which I could pretend they lived in a cave, and I their lone human connection. Each horse was its own being, each with its particular musculature over which light played from my bedroom window.

Together, the sum of the separate entities was more than its parts. On each was tied an invisible rope that tethered them to the word *horse*, the idea of *horse*, and to *horse* galloping through imagination's realm. The Fighting Stallion, the Arabian Stallion, Man O' War, the Mustang, the Bucking Bronco, the Running Foal. (Where were the mares? I had not yet approached that question.) The horses—the statues and the herds they represented—could be ordered in a number of ways depending on my need: by color, shade, size, attitude, breed, age. Some could be paired.

Others repelled one another like magnets, or as I found myself repelled by the idea of mathematical sets I was learning in school, even though I was unknowingly enacting them at home, with horses. Later, as I moved into adolescence, I would do the same thing with Troll dolls, who could be grouped by color of hair, length of hair, eye color, belly button, butt crack, and degree of evil, which my imagination supplied.

Maybe there is something to kid-level, to the way in which order and the imagination are not in binary opposition to each other but feed each other. Sugar cubes on an open hand.

II.

A careless shoe-string, in whose tie / I see a wild civility: / Do more bewitch me than when art / Is too precise in every part.
—Robert Herrick, "Delight in Disorder"

When I think of order, I think of disorder.

I began writing poems before I knew what poems were. There was no internet, no social media with its surfeit of poems to model, mock, and learn from. There were books, some of which entered my house via my mother when she went to college as an English major at age thirty-four after my father died.

She had built a bricks-and-boards bookcase in the living room, low to the ground, and there, sitting on the floor, I'd touch and read the books' spines. Chaucer. Shakespeare. The Romantic Period (I imagined kissing.), Whitman. Emerson. Melville. Hawthorne. Conrad. Joyce. A book with a gray spine and red type: *Modern Poetry*. I was old enough to know I was a girl, and young enough to absorb, without resistance, the fact that all of these names belonged to men. Where were the mares? That would come later.

My first poems sprang from the forehead of a manual typewriter in typing class, a high school requirement, as was home economics, for girls. They were single-spaced. The ink was ebony and bled with the pounding of the keys, or if the ribbon was shot, faded to dappled gray. The poems were unaware of a left margin and cascaded down the page with abandon. "Poem," to me, meant that within the margins of the typing paper I could pretty much do anything I wanted. I think I got this notion from my primary influence, rock 'n' roll. (I hadn't yet noticed how seamlessly songs of anarchy could be strung together into an album.)

There was little poetry taught in my high school English classes. In middle school, one teacher forced us to memorize and recite poems selected for us. Though I pretended to hate this exercise, as the other kids said they did, I secretly loved it. Sometimes I still hear those poems in my head: Sam Walter Foss's "There are hermit souls that live withdrawn in the peace of their self-content; there are souls, like stars, that dwell apart, in the fellowless firmament..." ("House by the Side of the Road"). I had no idea what a fellowless firmament was—but I wanted in. My favorite was Longfellow's "Paul Revere's Ride": "Listen, my children, and you shall hear of the midnight ride of Paul Revere, on the eighteenth of April, in Seventy-five, hardly a man is now alive, who remembers that famous day and year..." I could hear the hoofbeats in those cadences, which came back to me when I was trying to get to sleep at night or when I was really cooking on a typing class poem. These poems tuned my ear to metrical patterns in everyday life. The settings on the four burners of my mom's old stove, for instance, read this way: off high sim (simmer) low medium-low medium high. Thanks to Longfellow, I made a song of them in my head:

off, high, sim, low, medium-low, medium-high.
medium-high, medium-low, low, sim, high, off.

My first manuscript lived in a box. Actually, it was a cheap black briefcase. My father had used it when he attended college on the GI Bill after World War II, and now it was mine. Within its four worn corners I shoved all my treasures and necessities. Poems, spare change, tampons, matches, smokes, and a tiny pot of gooey Yardley lip gloss that gave my mouth the appearance of glass. The briefcase accompanied me to college, about sixty miles north of my hometown, where I majored in theater, and then anthropology, and finally English, before I stopped going to classes and was kicked out, but not before finishing my senior project, an eighty-poem manuscript in a black folder that I called *The Midnight Ride of Monster Woman* ("On the 8th of April in '77 / up she jump / into the saddle / she a tattle tale / and her skin / are green / and one if by land and two if by sea and three if by three if by three if by three...").

The briefcase joined me, my fake snakeskin suitcase which housed my clothes, and my manual typewriter on a train to New York City, where I was traveling to become a poet. I didn't know what it was to be a poet, but I'd absorbed the message that to become a poet one must leave the hinterlands, and so I left the hinterlands and proceeded to live a profoundly disorganized life. If high school was rock 'n' roll, New York was punk, odd jobs, love, addiction, violence, and self-estrangement. In a sense, it was living the poem rather than writing it. Nothing much ended up on the page in those years, but my life in New York became the fodder my mare would chew on for the rest of her days.

III.

Take Emily's 'Herbarium' far enough, and you have her.
—Richard B. Sewell (11)

When I think of order, I think of Emily Dickinson.

Before the poems came the herbarium, a collection of 424 pressed plants and flowers, a project she began when she was about the same age I was when I turned from horses to trolls. It was not terribly unusual for an adolescent girl in Dickinson's time and situation to construct an herbarium. In an 1845 letter, she urges her friend, Abiah Root, to compose one: "Have you made an herbarium yet? I hope you will if you have not, it would be such a treasure to you; 'most all the girls are making one'" (Onion). Yet, as one might imagine, Dickinson's herbarium out-herbariumed all the rest.

When I visited the house in Amherst where she lived her days and took her last breath, where she gardened and baked and wrote letters and poems, sometimes composing out loud when she skimmed the milk (Chiasson), I was able to browse a facsimile of the herbarium, the pages meticulously composed, a hybrid of botany and art, each pressed blossom and leaf a testimony to permanent impermanence, an emblem of the activity of wandering, looking, discovering, and gathering.

There seems to be no overt order to the collection, the plants not arranged, usually, by family (though there is a page devoted to various kinds of violets), color, or date of discovery. To my eye, the composition was primarily aesthetic and pragmatic. Pragmatic in that certain plants fit together spatially upon the page, and aesthetic in that each has a composed artfulness, a fluidity of movement, a suggestion of connection between the plants that is less analytical than intuitive. Emily has labeled each plant, sometimes with its common name, at other times with its scientific classification, in that beautiful, barely decipherable handwriting. The pages themselves are untitled, like her poems. And nowhere on the herbarium is Emily's name.

There is a through line from the herbarium to Dickinson's fascicles, her forty self-bound manuscripts, sewn at the spine with needle and thread. Like the poems themselves, like Emily herself, the fascicles have been taken apart, reassembled, fought over, and contemplated by scholars for generations. In the attempt to discern the poems' chronology, her handwriting has been analyzed, the paper, dated. What was Dickinson's purpose in binding a selection of poems this way? Of binding poems at all?

What was the meaning of the fascicles' ordering?

Like the herbarium, there is no overt principle of arrangement. If the poems are bound by subject or theme, the connections between poems are not obvious. They do not appear to be overtly linked by date or season. Some have suggested their order is utterly random, that the purpose of the binding was to "tidy up" (Cameron 140). Others have gone so far as to say that the indeterminacy itself was Dickinson's intention, or that the fascicles challenge the notion that the poem is a discrete entity. What if the fascicle allowed Dickinson the Experimenter—"Dickinson was an experimental gardener, working on projects such as trying to create a double nasturtium. She forced bulbs and kept tropical plants blooming all year in the conservatory, even when it meant staying up all night on very cold nights to tend the fires so flowers wouldn't freeze"—another avenue for improvisation, for opening up the text to hybridity (Steinbeck)?

What is a *fascicle*? A nerve bundle.

A flower cluster.
A work published in installments.

IV.

> *Then she stabbed them and bound them with string.*
> —Sharon Cameron (139)

When I think of order, I imagine Emily Dickinson at her little desk, recopying poems by lamplight.

Poetry is such a strange art, the poems an expression of solitude even as they reach toward an invisible reader. Who did a woman poet in nineteenth-century New England imagine reaching toward? Who do any of the marginalized imagine reaching toward? Maybe, as plants grow in the direction of the sun, the reaching is an act of survival, more instinct than strategy. But that conclusion is sentimental and limited, especially when considering a poet as playful and intellectually vigorous as Dickinson.

Maybe she was, indeed, tidying (such a woman-y-word), bringing the poems from briefcase to folder. Maybe arranging the poems in groups, stabbing, and sewing them, gave her a hint of the feeling of completion that publishing a book might have provided. Was she imagining future readers? Did this poet who sometimes supplied variants of words within the poems themselves, who sought serendipity, who allowed for triple meanings and cross-purposes, leave breadcrumbs for us to follow into just how experimental, enigmatic, and fluid a book's order might be? Might your book's arrangement, *taken far enough,* be you?

V.

> *Bound—a trouble—* / *And lives can bear it!* / *Limit—how deep a*
> *bleeding go!*
> —Emily Dickinson, "Bound—a Trouble"

When I think of order, I think of my first book, published when I was forty-two.

It is almost easier for me to connect with Emily Dickinson stabbing her fascicles than the woman I was in 1998 when my first book came out.

We have many selves. It's hard to remember what things looked like through the eyeholes of the ones we cast aside.

I had been writing poems for nearly three decades but hadn't thought much about publishing, to be honest. Again, we were not yet living in internet time. Broadcasting oneself, let alone self-branding, was not a standard. Nor was ambition, at least where I am from. I had to learn ambition, like learning to apply eyeliner. There were famous poets. Most were white men. Some were generous. Many were dismissive or self-indulgent, showing up to their own readings plastered and hitting on everyone in the front row.

The poems had accompanied me back to the Midwest from New York, when I finally got the guts to leave, and through graduate school, where I got a degree in social work. I then practiced in a domestic assault shelter, a community mental health center (one of my specialties was window peekers), an alternative health clinic, and in my own small private practice above a feminist bookstore. I was married, parenting a son, and teaching part-time, first social work courses, then creative writing workshops at the college where I had been an undergraduate, the one that had booted me more than a decade earlier. I wasn't hiding my poems, not by any means. I gave readings. Taught workshops. Although I wrote poems all the time, poetry was less of a career than a side dish, at least for people like me. Who were people like me? Well, a person from the rural Midwest. A teacher, a social worker, but not an academic. A wrong person. Looked wrong. Acted wrong. Talked wrong. "How are you doing?" a professor might ask. "I'm doing good," I'd answer. It would slip out before I could self-correct.

A relatively famous fiction writer lived, at that time, in my neighborhood. He often biked by my house wearing an electric blue cycling bodysuit. One day he stopped at the base of my driveway as I was struggling to get my son in his car seat. "Publishing anything?" he asked. "I'm writing a lot but not really sending anything out," I answered. "What's the plan?" he asked (I'd say sneeringly, but I rarely use adverbs), the lenses of his wire-rim glasses reflecting the white sky. "Are you going to be another Emily Dickinson and hide your poems under the bed?" The humiliation I felt, like the flies that land on the faces of farm animals, was so familiar I barely noticed it. Looking back, I am amused at how often I have heard or read the urban legend that Dickinson hid her poems under her bed, in her underwear drawer, or under a cabbage leaf, as if the lack of visibility of her work was her fault, an outgrowth of her eccentricity, rather than a result of the deficiency of inroads to publication for women in the nineteenth century, even white, white-clad women like Emily Dickinson.

I had published exactly eleven poems in six magazines when the editor of a new press came calling. The press was born in the town I lived in, so he was aware that I existed. I'd even taken a writing course with him once, long ago, and he had called me a "feminist tiger" in class. I'm not sure it was a compliment. Somehow over the years he had come around and asked to look at a manuscript. I had poems all over the place, but nothing that looked like a manuscript. What was a manuscript? I gathered together poems that felt like they might cohere and began to think about order.

Looking at the book now—I haven't really held it in my hands for a decade or more, but I hold it now—I find I quite like what I composed, guided by instinct rather than craft, or maybe an instinct for craft. It's the horse statue instinct, the herbarium instinct. The spine of the book is tattered. The cover art, about which I had no say, once magenta, now faded to pink, features a rowboat, a young, blonde woman who seems to be naked, and a butcher knife stabbing downward, on which the title precipitously balances. *It Blows You Hollow*. Feminist tiger indeed.

The first section grounds the reader in the apparently personal, and in landscape, and then, through a sequence of God poems, introduces a speaker who would evolve through all of the books I've written since. Blasphemous. Ironically, even comically, erotic. In the second section I now see the origins of something headier—a kind of largesse that lifts the poems off into ideas enacted with more rhetorical oomph. The third and final section is a sequence I wrote on an island in Lake Huron, staying in a borrowed cabin. I remember her—that self—best. Well enough that I can almost claim her. Even though I'd only be away for a few weeks I remember driving away from my husband and son with a grief I could almost not stomach and heading north on what felt like a pilgrimage, crossing the Mackinac Bridge to Hendrix's "The Wind Cries Mary," taking a car ferry to the island. Alone. Alone. The poems fell under the influence of the dead, who would become my guides in my proceeding books. Kevin Young writes in his essay "Deadism" of "a poetry that speaks from the mouths of those gone that aren't really gone, a poetry of ghosts and haunts. Of haints: not ain'ts" (191). Since earliest childhood I had been aligned with the dead. My time on the island, separated from the comforts of the domestic realm, simply made that alignment more apparent.

It Blows You Hollow unfolds in a simple but worthy trajectory. And in the final section, a foreshadowing. The aloneness would stick. Within a month after I received the heavy box of finished books, without warning or explanation, my husband left. Now, even the words "my husband" seem strange. Had I really been a wife? Lining up the spice jars? By alphabet? By heat?

VI.

> *The first issue is always one of self-knowledge or self-recognition. Once a poet has a sense of his or her fundamental temperament, the possibilities for growth are twofold. The first is to go further into the gift, but such a decision carries with it the risk of a narrowing as well as the promise of a deepening. The second direction is to expand.*
> —Gregory Orr, "Four Temperaments and the Forms of Poetry" (36)

When I think of order, I think of the temperaments.

In Gregory Orr's "Four Temperaments and the Forms of Poetry," he proposes that all poets enact one of four core temperaments in their work— story, structure, music, or imagination. Story and structure, he writes, are limiting impulses. Music and imagination, conversely, represent an impulse for limitlessness. Each of us is in our sweet spot within one of the four temperaments. To grow as a poet, Orr suggests, is to walk across the lane and integrate one of the opposing temperaments. If you are primarily a story or structure poet, for instance, walk in the direction of music or imagination. If you reside in music or imagination, bring story or structure to the party.

My mentor, Conrad Hilberry, was a structure poet. "As long as the form comes out right," he told me, "I'm perfectly happy, even if it doesn't express much!" Then he laughed like a crow. I never read any of his poems that didn't express much, but yes, structure was his pleasure and his jam. His work was at its most edgy when he walked toward imagination or music, as he increasingly did in the second half of his writing life. I am primarily an imagination poet. The danger, of course, is meandering. Self-indulging. When I walk toward story or structure the poems gain ballast. Accessibility. In walking toward each other, Conrad and I lived Orr's template.

There is something to be said for a boundary. There is also something to be said for unbinding. Ask anyone who has ever worn a bra.

I'm wondering if the same could be said for a book manuscript. If your poems tend toward the limiting impulses of story or structure, might you arrange the manuscript to spark musical or imaginative energy, steering clear, for instance, of overt linear order? If you're in the music or imagination camp, could you try shaping your book with an eye toward structural and/or narrative coherence?

Boundedness is an act of identity, of what Orr calls "self-recognition." The book is this and not that. It is not everything. It is *this* thing. It has, in fact, a thesis, just like your life does if you have the guts to look. Maybe the binding, the thesis, the order all shore us up against death. At least as a container for death. Maybe unbinding is to open our arms to death (and grief and Eros and hallucination), to forces that can't be compressed, denied, or contained. To chaos. To the guidance of the dead. (Etched on my father's headstone, "Guidance," and a torch.)

"Batter my heart, three-person'd God, for you / As yet but knock, breathe, shine, and seek to mend; / That I may rise and stand, o'erthrow me, and bend / Your force to break, blow, burn, and make me new," John Donne writes in the most notorious of his Holy Sonnets. Only the sonnet's structure can hold Donne's wrestling with God, the ravishing by God. Without the huff and chuff of imagination, the wrestling and ravishing, the sonnet is a tree locust shell, a carcass unhaunted by a soul.

VII.

A woman in the shape of a monster / a monster in the shape of a woman / the skies are full of them.
—Adrienne Rich, "Planetarium"

When I think about order, I think about monsters.

It would be twelve years after *It Blows You Hollow*—not for lack of trying—before I got a second book into the world, *Wolf Lake, White Gown*

Blown Open. The first book, pink cover, butcher knife, and all, had taught me to have ambition for my work. Writing poems, and binding them into something like wholeness, even a wholeness that reflected the implosion of the life I knew, the life my son knew, became the singular occupation, outside of earning a living and raising Dylan, that gave me a sense of a future. It is often the case, don't ask me why, that spouses, partners, lovers need to construct the person they are leaving as well worth leaving. Maybe it's an act of self-justification, a way to live with themselves. Maybe calling home your projections requires a kind of violence. When he broke up with me, my first boyfriend, in seventh grade, made a papier-mâché sculpture of me in art class with the word "Monster" scrawled in white paint over the hulking black form. My husband left me with little but this: he told me he had secretly considered me, for years, a monster. This would inspire in me not the wish to prove him otherwise, but as Orr writes, "to go further into the gift" of my monstrousness, not through monstrous deeds but through ferocity—of imagination, empathy, audacity, fealty to the craft.

I'd always been a freak, hadn't I? "Little Touch-Me-Not," the kids called me. Laid on my belly and stared for hours into the ice fishing hole. Tasted the bitter milk of milkweed pods. Followed the woman draped always in black into the next-door cemetery to listen to her talk to her dead. "As future skinned animals, to go to schools we must pass before a butcher shop, through the slaughter, to the cemetery door," writes Hélène Cixous, quoting Thomas Bernard (8). Saved seven times in damp, cement block churches. Obsessed with the mortician's kids and his craft. A freak, as had been my mother before me—Joyce-reading widow with a crazy laugh. My mother who, as a kid, slept on sugar sacks in the basement to have privacy. Who walked barefoot around an inland lake and stepped by accident into the coil of a snake. It laid its fangs in. No one would believe her. My mother who, upon dropping the cherry pie on Thanksgiving, said "fuck it" and scraped it off the floor and served it. A free, uncategorizable woman. Now I was Monster Woman with a limp, after a fortuitous accident, and poetry my consort. The barn was on fire. The mares rampaged through the meadow.

Every time an editor passed on the manuscript (let's not call it rejection—too psychological), it sharpened my resolve and the intensity of my self-critique. I got rid of poems, added new ones, and rethought the book's sectioning. One editor at a regional press responded only, "Too many divorce poems!" As pissed as I was, I took it to heart. Rather than eradicating divorce from the book—I mean, it was my reality—I raised its presence, and my speaker's presence, to what my friend Gail Griffin, in a poem, calls "a bigger bigness" (7). The book's shape lifted off into something like allegory, and that lesson followed me into all the books that have followed, and into the life that followed.

One eye on the road, one on the sky, or something like that.

The iteration of the book that James Tate selected for the Juniper Prize had been ordered and reordered with each wave of rebuffs. What finally resulted felt, well, right. Somehow finished in the way it hadn't before. There is an arc to the sections, as I look at them now, from origins, to the establishment of a complex speaker, a kind of jaded trickster, to allegories of erotic loss, to landscape erotics, to—something like philosophy, a rhetoric of loss, an "art of losing" without the villanelle. Simply put, the book dominoed from what made me to what happened to me to what I did with it. I'd also titled the sections rather than simply numbering them using only lowercase letters, and added a parenthetical phrase to each title: I. "the river burrs (and burns)," II. "we were happy (we were unclean)," III. "lost my baby (almost lost my mind)," IV. "paper heron (painted blue)," V. "quick needle (silver light)." Something about that system of titling brought an improvisational energy to the collection that carries over into the whole experience of reading it.

Another decision I'd made about this final version, the one that somehow clicked, was a rethinking of what poem the reader should encounter first. I shifted from a "big" poem to a smaller, sonnet-length poem. "Jesus wept and so did Rowena Lee" is clear in intent, and emotionally available. It establishes the book's setting, people, class, language, and theology. It Bibles the working class, and women, and Jesuses human suffering. I can see that now. At the time I couldn't have explained why it worked. I was running on instinct and the education that comes from a bullish combination of failure and persistence. Tate's single editorial suggestion was to retitle the book from *The River Purrs and Burns* to *Wolf Lake, White Gown Blown Open*. He was undoubtedly right. The new title carried the sonic and image DNA of the whole collection. And my white gown *was* blown open, wasn't it?

VIII.

But in the act of making a poem at least two crucial things have taken place that are different from ordinary life. First, we have shifted the crisis to a bearable distance from us: removed it to the symbolic but vivid world of language. Secondly, we have actively made and shaped this model of our situation rather than passively endured it as lived experience.
—Gregory Orr, *Poetry as Survival* (4)

When I think of order, I think of taking hold.

The ensuing books, *Four-Legged Girl, Still Life with Two Dead Peacocks and a Girl,* and *frank: sonnets,* each represent and perform a step along a footpath toward my evolution as a person and a poet. I no longer lived poem to poem, but book to book. What is the next necessary move? What have I not yet considered? What are my intellectual concerns *now*, my theoretical concerns, my formal concerns, my spiritual concerns? How do I extend myself rather than imitate myself? What have I yet to tell?

These are questions that cannot be answered by crowdsourcing, nor ultimately by the examples of what others did or are doing. The path is made visible, for me anyway, in solitude ("there are souls, like stars, that dwell apart, in the fellowless firmament…"), and there are no shortcuts. It is what Gregory Orr calls, in the introduction to his book *Poetry as Survival,* the "active taking-hold of one's emotional life"(5).

And yet. And yet I was no longer fully alone in my work. My publisher was now Graywolf Press, my editor, Jeff Shotts. There is no greater provocation to risk than to be taken seriously, not just by attitude but by pen. To have the poems proofed within an inch of their lives, pored over. To have the manuscript's movement considered critically. To write—not *for* someone—but *toward* someone. An objective other who knows their shit. We literary types have memorized the story, Dickinson's first letter to Thomas Wentworth Higginson, the person who would become her somewhat objective other: "Are you too deeply occupied to say if my Verse is alive?" So coy! So performed. And yet I understand the need for someone unobtrusive but honest now that my wish has been met.

In *Four-Legged Girl* I was still amassing poems without a particular thesis in mind. The book's frame was revealed and clarified in the act of arranging the manuscript over time. The final ordering, grappled with over years, reveals a plotline which I consider a girl-picaresque. Section I, "blossomhouse," begins in a rural childhood lush with loss, foliage, and imagination, and ends in a coming of age. Section II, "blowtorch the hinges," the book's original title and a Whitman reference, lifts off into the urban, and into addictive, erotic love. Section III, "lush," is composed of one eight-page poem, "I can't listen to music, especially 'Lush Life'," which Jeff suggested should serve as the book's hub. It is a lyric paean to my relationship with a drug addict, in conversation with Lorca's "Romance Sonámbulo" and Billy Strayhorn's song, "Lush Life." Section IV, "free beer," is a kind of autopsy of loss and desire. The final section returns to the rural, but now via mythic memory. It ends with self-reinvention, akin to Plath's "out of the ash I rise with my red hair." In my case, it is the dismantling of beauty and the claiming of the four-legged girl, the holy freak.

Still Life with Two Dead Peacocks and a Girl is probably the most consciously *made* book I've written so far. It began when I woke from a dream in which the words "still life" were emblazoned in the dark space behind my eyes. From there, because I trust in dreams, I did research and began to theorize the intersection of still life painting, often seen as a lesser visual art than paintings of religion or history, and the rural place and people that made me. Although much of the content is personal, the book's purposes are aesthetic and cultural. It asks questions about the gaze, about who looks and who is looked upon, about the Eden of art and who has access to it, and those questions unfolded in the ordering of the manuscript. The sections are no longer numbered but are marked by fragments of the title painting, Rembrandt's *Still Life with Two Dead Peacocks and a Girl*. The whole book is framed by two bookend poems, "I Have Lived My Whole Life in a Painting Called *Paradise*" and "I Climbed Out of a Painting Called *Paradise*," modeled, in a sense, on Bruegel's peasant landscapes.

The book also contains formal experimentation, first, with what Ginsberg called American Sentences—seventeen syllables, akin to haiku, but without line breaks—and my own invention, sonnets in which each line is seventeen syllables.

This aspect of *Peacocks* would guide me into my next book, *frank: sonnets*, a sort of memoir in 127 contemporary sonnets. Despite its adherence to the form, the arrangement of the book itself is relatively simple. The poems appear not in the order of their living but in the order of their making, so that I could capture the improvisational nature of memory. Although I originally had divided the poems into titled sections, Jeff suggested we get rid of those, that the trajectory represent a seamless cascade rather than something divided into movements. Now I can't imagine it any other way. The units of the sonnet, all fourteen lines, some gesturing toward rhyme and meter, others not, all hold the same amount of space, the same pressure, like hospital windows, or cells in a film strip. Nothing is more foreground or background than anything else. Strung together, the sonnets compose a book that theorizes memory and converses with the dead. Do they compose, also, a life? Some might say so.

All the mares of my days, each fourteen hands high, lined up in a restless herd.

IX.

> *Since then—'tis Centuries—and yet / Feels shorter than the Day / I first surmised the Horses' Heads / Were toward Eternity—*
> —Emily Dickinson, "Because I could not stop for Death"

I believe you could take apart this essay, cut it with dull scissors, section from section like a horsetail weed, reconstitute it in a different order, stab it, and bind it anew. In this way, I have wanted to enact the thesis in my structure. Although I have been apparently personal here, I have been selective. I have not told everything. I've left out the really gruesome parts and have kept only that which might serve the argument. This is what we do in poems, in books, in all works of art. The omissions shape the work as much as the presences.

I hope you—you, poet—have taken away from this experiment that order is a birthright, as is disorder. In your way, not in mine, you've done it all of your life. No one has to teach it to you. You need only remember. There is no correct way to order your manuscript except for the way that most reflects your self-recognition. To get there may require that you develop an intimate relationship with loneliness. A deeper kinship with the restless herd of the dead.

In writing and ordering your poems, you are forging a self. Housing it in a stall of your own making. You are building a bearable myth. You are constructing, as much in your process as your product, some fragment of the everlasting.

Works Cited

Cameron, Sharon. "Dickinson's Fascicles." *Dickinson's Fascicles: A Spectrum of Possibilities*, edited by Paul Crumbley and Eleanor Elson Heginbotham. Ohio University Press, 2014, pp. 12–32.

Chiasson, Dan. "Emily Dickinson's Singular Scrap Poetry." *The New Yorker*, 27 Nov. 2016, https://www.newyorker.com/magazine/2016/12/05/emily-dickinsons-singular-scrap-poetry. Accessed 22 Nov. 2021.

Cixous, Hélène. *Three Steps on the Ladder of Writing*. Columbia University Press, 1994.

Dickinson, Emily. "Because I could not stop for Death." *Poetry Foundation*, https://www.poetryfoundation.org/poems/47652/because-i-could-not-stop-for-death-479. Accessed 22 Nov. 2021.

Dickinson, Emily. "Bound—a Trouble." *AllPoetry.com*, https://allpoetry.com/Bound--a-trouble. Accessed 22 Nov. 2021.

Donne, John. "Holy Sonnets: Batter my heart, three-person'd God." *Poetry Foundation*, https://www.poetryfoundation.org/poems/44106/holy-sonnets-batter-my-heart-three-persond-god. Accessed 22 Nov. 2021.

Foss, Sam Walter. "A House by the Side of the Road." *AllPoetry.com*, https://allpoetry.com/The-House-By-The-Side-Of-The-Road. Accessed 22 Nov. 2021.

Griffin, Gail. "Ninth Grade Social Studies Lesson." *Cauldron*, Kalamazoo College, 1998, https://cache.kzoo.edu/bitstream/handle/10920/30798/1988Cauldr onSummer.pdf. Accessed 23 Nov. 2021.

Harjo, Joy. "She Had Some Horses." *Poetry Foundation*, https://www.poetryfoundation.org/poems/141852/she-had-some-horses-590104cf40742. Accessed 22 Nov. 2021.

Herrick, Robert. "Delight in Disorder." *Poetry Foundation*, https://www.poetryfoundation.org/poems/47285/delight-in-disorder. Accessed 22 Nov. 2021.

Longfellow, Henry Wadsworth. "Paul Revere's Ride." *Poets.org*, https://poets.org/poem/paul-reveres-ride. Accessed 22 Nov. 2021.

Onion, Rebecca. "A Teenage Emily Dickinson's Collection of Dried Flowers." *Slate*, 4 June 2013, https://slate.com/human-interest/2013/06/emily-dickinson-her-collection-of-botanical-specimens-photos.html. Accessed 22 Nov. 2021.

Orr, Gregory. "Four Temperaments and the Forms of Poetry." *The American Poetry Review*, vol. 17, no. 5, 1988, pp. 33–36.

Rich, Adrienne. "Planetarium." *Poetry Foundation*, https://www.poetryfoundation.org/poems/46568/planetarium-56d2267df376c. Accessed 22 Nov. 2021.

Sewell, Richard B. "Science and the Poet: Emily Dickinson's Herbarium and 'The Clue Divine.'" *Harvard Library Bulletin*, vol. 3, no. 1, 1992, pp. 11–26.

"Sharon Olds: Blood, Sweat and Fears." *The Independent*, 27 Oct. 2006, https://www.independent.co.uk/arts-entertainment/books/features/sharon-olds-blood-sweat-and-fears-421691.html. Accessed 23 Nov. 2021.

Steinbeck, Diane. "In Emily Dickinson's Garden." *The Morning Call*, 22 Sept. 2006. https://www.mcall.com/news/mc-xpm-2006-09-22-3678617-story.html. Accessed 22 Nov. 2021.

Young, Kevin. "Poetics Statement: from On Deadism." *American Poets in the 21st Century: The New Poetics*, edited by Claudia Rankine and Lisa Sewell. Wesleyan University Press, 2007, pp. 190–192.

Poems as Paintings
Life-Drawing in Words

Heather Treseler

I. Trapdoor

THE FIRST TIME I felt a metaphor in my body I was four years old. It was a sweltering day in June, and I sat behind a wooden desk that seemed as large as a ship's prow. I was swinging my feet, pleasurably, from a tall chair as my father read from James Joyce's "The Dead" to his students at Dedham High School: students two or three times my size, their legs stretching enviably all the way to the floor. Too shy to look at teenagers directly, I studied shoes—high-tops, sandals, penny loafers, mules—and dust motes, falling in a window's shaft of light.

"Snow was general all over Ireland," my father's voice intoned. "It was falling…on the treeless hills…upon the Bog of Allen…softly falling into the dark mutinous Shannon waves" (Joyce 255). Damp heat glued my legs to the wooden chair, but I imagined dust motes as snowflakes falling inside and outside of the building, a carpet of white over the waxed floor, the gangly teenagers, a US flag beside the fire alarm, and the chrome on cars parked outdoors, wincing in the sunlight.

Snow was general all over Ireland. And all over Dedham, Massachusetts, a modest town which, in its elite section, housed an estate deemed fit to be the governor's mansion. A blue-collar suburb of carpenters, plumbers, teamsters, and electricians, Dedham—in all its summer dust—became, in my mind, Dublin in a wintry snow. I felt the metaphor intensely, as an electric charge or an ocean wave tossed across my body. It thrilled me that language could alter my sense of person and place, climate and consequence.

My father was leaving his job as a high school English teacher because he had to make more money. Perhaps he brought me to his classroom to show me his profession before he left it. I felt the sadness of this departure: his withdrawing from a world in which his identity had been staked, performed, and rewarded. I sensed that I, too, would be forced to leave places or people I loved. It filled me with foreboding, a funereal feeling not yet matured to grief.

As we walked the deserted halls of Dedham High late that afternoon, I tucked my small hand into my father's reassuring one. Passing glass cases of sports trophies in the high school lobby, I caught my reflection. Contrails of white chalk dust twirled down my cardigan, overalls, and red shoes. Chalk, and the remnants of written words, had smudged me from head to toe and caked my father's wide hand like a gymnast's before he vaults onto a pommel horse.

Chalk and summer dust were general all over Dedham.

My father pushed against the weighty school doors and I followed him, feeling a gush of hot air against my face as we stepped outside. The doors swung shut behind us. In some part of my four-year-old brain, I resolved to come back to this place my father was being forced to abandon: a place of written words and stories read aloud. A place of trapdoor metaphors. A country of language in which you could, in an instant, go somewhere, be someone else.

II. Supposed Person

By eighteen, I was someone else. Someone trying to write—haltingly, poorly, stubbornly—good poems. The capacity of language to make pictures, to transform the often lackluster world into something of worth remained sacred to me, long after my adolescent skepticism had skewered almost everything else.

When I encountered Joyce's story again, in a college seminar, it seemed less about the triumph of metaphor and more about the startling discovery of an alienating gap within a marriage. Joyce's married couple, the Conroys, have been living out that institution's fiction of comprehensive knowledge of another human being. At eighteen, this already seemed a romanticized notion, one as old as Eden, wagered against the cost of fruit and the wrath of a god. Alienation, even within intimacy, seemed a more certain bet, although I knew little then about love or the fidelity of a long friendship, one that spans decades, growing to accommodate individuals' separateness: how, like subatomic particles, we have already changed once someone has begun to approximate our true dimensions.

Joyce's story alchemized once I read it myself. But what had not changed—between the ages of four and eighteen—was my twinned attraction to visual art and literature, an affinity that would, over time, become a strategy in my writing. My mother had taken the four of us, as children, to museums and galleries in the Boston area, dosing us in "high culture" and allowing us to study whatever appealed to us. Something from these secular baptisms took: as a child, I found myself cast under a spell in front of a painting or sculpture, much the way a story or poem held my total attention.

When I felt homesick as a college freshman, I instinctively retreated to the local museum. There, gazing at a giant Buddha or a Greek kouros boy, an Edwardian mantelpiece or a sculpture by Louise Bourgeois, I had the sensation of being physically held, static but also charged, warmed. The psychoanalyst Christopher Bollas asserts that a work of art can hold its viewer the way a parent holds a child (386). We see—and are recognized—by the psyche emanating from the painted canvas or sculpted form. As I began to write, two realms trafficked in my head, language calling up visual image and material art turning my hand reflexively to the page. In her treatise *On Beauty*, Elaine Scarry asserts that beauty spurs production *and* reproduction, our aesthetic instinct parallel to sexual drive (4–5). If the urge to make art is akin to libidinal desire, I found among beautiful things a family feeling. In museums, we are surrounded by offspring.

The Horatian simile, *ut pictura poesis*, "as in painting as in poetry," made complete sense to me, as did the statement of the original author of that observation, Simonides of Keos who, in Plutarch's account, asserts that "poetry is a speaking picture, painting a silent poetry" (Larrabee 881–2). More than once a week, I frequented the Rhode Island School of Design's museum, gathering sparks of light and color that I took back to a concrete room on the third floor of the university library where adaptive technology and furniture allowed me to read and write.

An accident in adolescence had left me invisibly but substantially injured. I spent much of my college years lying face down: reading, writing, and translating on a converted massage table with an aperture that allowed me to view books tucked beneath it. By my senior year, I had drafted two manuscripts—in poetry and fiction—which, unpublished, would none-theless scaffold my career as a writer. I was creating a body of words distinct from my physical self and the vulnerability I felt as a slight and incapaci-tated woman, no longer able to run or, seemingly, fight back against an assailant. Leaving the library after midnight, I scurried back to my dorm room, exhilarated by my bookish excursions but alert to moving shadows.

For many years, I was a shade of myself, haunted by a regressive shyness as I found ways to mitigate physical limitations and imitate the confidence of the uninjured. Walking through Providence, I found a flyer seeking a model for a cohort of artists, practicing their life-drawing skills. I answered it. Serving as a model became one of my odd jobs as a scholarship student, paying for my own books and pizza. Ironically, it was the one zone in which my acute self-consciousness disappeared. As a static subject, I was an aesthetic challenge: a set of geometric planes and coloration to affix to canvas or paper.

Heating pipes rattled, hissed, and sighed like cantankerous old lovers in the perpetually overheated studio, and I slipped into a sleepy daydream: a meditative state in warm humid air. Subtle sounds of brush or pencil on paper, adjustments of easels, and murmurs of artists listening to headphones or conferring quietly lent the room an intentional focus such as I had felt in the chapel of Franciscan nuns who taught at my grade school. I could have been back there, among the older women of long habits, their rosaries in rotary prayer.

Modeling gave me an ease in embodiment I did not experience else-where. As a competitive athlete before my accident, I was focused on strength, racing speed, and time. But as an artist's subject, the fact of my imperfect body was a given. I did not need to race around a track at break-neck pace or spend hours in a weight room, quickening my muscles. I had only to arrive, wearing my face as it had awoken that day. Unlike the catcallers on city streets or the aggressive appraisers at local bars, these studio artists were exacting of *themselves*. My body was provocation, not invitation, and part of an artistic process.

Among visual artists, I found my tribe. I had none of their skill, but I was deeply intrigued by what they could telegraph between eye and hand. And their casual rivalry was unlike the frank paranoia among creative writing students in the late '90s, who feigned an affected casualness or practiced a cutthroat cliquishness linked to some notion of "relevance." Literary arts, around the millennium, were suffering as the internet reshaped the marketplace for books and journalism. My fellow writing students were, with exception, an anxious jealous bunch, whereas visual artists seemed playful, unabashed. I learned to love the smell of graphite and turpentine.

One artist, training to be a psychiatrist and a portraitist, became my roommate for three years: we shared a walk-up a half-mile from campus beside a raucous fraternity. Ignoring our neighbors' backyard beer pong, we filled the sunny apartment with books, plants, and artwork. I was also my roommate's subject on occasion. One drawing, which she sketched over many weeks, was completed as I worked at my desk. The likeness of my face, then and now, is startlingly accurate—high coloring, deep laugh lines, green eyes, a messy corona of brown hair. In profile, I am looking into the near distance, elsewhere.

Being sketched by a close friend remains one of my most intimate experiences of attention. Although, in those hours, her hands did not physically engage with my body—there was no lover's caress or surgeon's incision—I felt profoundly held, recognized, even provisionally healed. Figurative touch can be as memorable as haptic occasion. As a poet, I shape language, hoping to give readers an anatomy of words, a relation to the figure in the frame: someone "drawn from life" who is not me, as Emily Dickinson wrote, but a "supposed person" (*Selected Letters* 176).

Meanwhile, poems by people I have never met play insistently in mind alongside the garrulity of inner chatter. We are radios of alternating frequencies, traveling in and out of reception zones; we are galleries of tableaux we have not ourselves made. This is the largesse of art, which spares us the chronic bewilderment of raw experience. As in painting, as in poetry, we draw from "life models" real and imagined. We scale what we have known of lack and abundance, joy, and suffering down to the size of the human eye, ear, and reach of understanding.

III. Mare and Mirror

At an artists' residency in the foothills of the Blue Ridge Mountains, I met an older poet, one married to a painter, and noticed that he had tacked his manuscript in its hypothetical order around the four walls of his studio. This way, he explained, he could see it whole and, with scotch tape, make adjustments. I studied his gallery, his poems arranged like miniature unframed canvases. As I turned toward the third wall, a horse's head suddenly appeared in the window: it was the mare I had seen earlier, grazing in the meadow. She looked intrigued by the poet's ad hoc museum. For a moment, we studied each other, the window frame turning each of us into a portrait for the other. She looked curious, her chestnut brown eyes taking in the whole scene. I wondered what, if anything, she saw in me, a biped on the other side of the glass.

I had earned tenure at the age of thirty-seven, and I finally felt secure. Worried after college that I might become an actual starving artist, I had worked three jobs as a copywriter, nurse's aide, and teacher while applying to funded doctoral programs. I figured I could earn a PhD in literature while writing poems. Midway through the doctoral program, it occurred to me that I needed to prove my nettle as a literary scholar. So I did and, against terrible odds, I landed a tenure-track position.

But between the ages of twenty-four and thirty-seven, I was in a professional sprint. I wrote poems in the margins. For a while, the more work I did as a critic, the more poems seemed to pop up like toast. That catalytic conversion slowed once I began teaching at a state university where I had four courses a semester and about eighty students and advisees. I felt like Mother Hubbard who had so many (collegiate) children, she didn't know what to do.

In those years, there was little time for my own literary production or, it turned out, reproduction. There was no shoulder on the freeway. When I wasn't teaching or grading, I slept. On weekends, I wrote bits of scholarship and literary journalism, but I did not have energy for poems. There was no time to daydream, to read without pedagogical purpose, or to take walks without a wary eye on the clock. Tenured, I was almost no longer a poet.

Feeling desperate, I had traveled to a monastery-turned-artists' colony in rural Virginia hoping to salvage what might remain of that impulse, and I saw it on the walls of the older poet's studio and later, when I read his book in print: poems that had an arc, a set of teleological ties, a mix of congruence and counterpoint. Poems that, in their space and sound, were "speaking pictures," a gallery of sensibility.

I thought of lines in T. S. Eliot's "Ash Wednesday," that poem of yearning and disenchantment: "Speech without word and / word of no speech," in which he posits a communicative register beyond the materiality of language. It is a lofty, perhaps impossible goal for mere mortals, but it articulates the need that undergirds artistic endeavor. In his poem "Advice to the Players," Frank Bidart similarly asserts: "We are creatures who need to make. / ... / Making is the mirror in which we see ourselves. / ... not only large things, a family, a book, a business: / but the shape we give this afternoon, a conversation between / two friends, a meal" (346). Bidart suggests that the will to make animates not just dedicated artists, but all human beings, an instinct we betray at our peril.

The brown mare, without foal, who gazed at me through the window into a room of poems felt like a prescriptive omen: *follow your nature.* So I began writing poems again—at first badly. Then less so. When I felt distant from poems, I reviewed collections I admired. I hunted through archives, tracking how other poets drew from dreams and travels, animals and artifacts, paintings and songs, conversations and letters. When I could not plant a seed, I turned the soil.

IV. Family Feeling

Around this time, while giving a conference paper, I found a poetry brother, one who had trained with the same two poets who had been my mentors. We shared, in effect, artistic parents, and he was gentle and ambitious enough to be an ideal first reader. We began exchanging drafts. Shortly thereafter, at a seminar in the Elizabeth Bishop archive, I found three poetry sisters for whom Bishop's poems had distinctly different kinds of resonance. They too were carving out niches in their lives in which to write, shrugging off the overreach of professional and personal claims, a hard task for those often tapped to do the affective labor of workplaces and home places. An artist can be starved of more than food. Privacy and time, it turns out, are as necessary as calories, light, and heat.

At midlife, I had new siblings. I had "family feeling" without, in the traditional sense, having constructed a family. It was this constellation of friendships that anchored me as I dove into the poems I had drafted over the years and separated them into Jungian streams: poems having to do with visual art; poems that remixed classical myths; and poems related to girlhood, family travail, and New England history. Some had been published; some had even won awards. But I could not find, within them, the shape of a book. I could not, as Dickinson asserts, "see to see" (*Complete Poems* 224).

So I turned back to Horace's *Ars Poetica*, the poet's letter to his friends, one of the earliest poetry handbooks. In it, he puts forth his famous adage of *ut pictura poesis*, as well as his advice to let a finished poem mature for nine years before publication, a long probation especially for a Roman who lived for just fifty-six years (300). But I had forgotten Horace's emphasis on poems lending the reader a varied terrain of perspectives:

> As it is with a picture,
> So with a poem; one will attract you more
> The nearer you stand, another, the farther away.
> One likes the shadow, another will want to be seen
> In broad daylight, and has not fear of the critic
> With all his shrewd insight. One gives pleasure
> But once only; another will always give pleasure. (300)

Horace had written to his friends, the Pisos, with his advice, and I wrote to mine, asking for help. Which of my poems could withstand the critic's klieg light, the reader's bid for returning pleasure? One friend critiqued a provisional manuscript. Another selected two dozen poems, which tracked a female speaker making a home in the world. Curiously, these were all poems I wrote not knowing how each might end. Each was an epistemological excursion that began with a low hum or visual burr, sounds or images I could not dislodge from mind, what rankled in stray hours of day or night.

"A poem…begins as a lump in the throat," Robert Frost opined, to which I would add "or a splinter in the senses" (22). In these poems, I was thinking about America in the late days of empire. I was yearning for matrilineal wisdom about how to survive in fraught circumstances, perilous times. I was not writing what I knew or could neatly caption, but rather what I did not know about friends or lovers, about new conditions in familiar landscapes.

When these forays startled me, and they did, I reminded myself that someone as accomplished as Picasso got interesting not in his early "blue" or "red" periods of exquisite traditional technique but when his art approximated the disorderly horror of warfare, the taunt of thwarted love, and the complex chaos of the self: in other words, when the material got beyond him, taxing and nearly surpassing his skill. For women and others who have been encouraged to think that their perspectives should keep to the restrictive cubbyholes of class origin or family story, professional pedigree, or public identity, it is a Joycean leap, an act of willful imagination to depart from an expected persona or cultural demesne. Ideally, birthright does not delimit the territory of imagination, and one's family—of friends, of affinities—can be chosen. As in paintings, poems can allow reader and writer, both, to be someone and somewhere else.

V. Gallery

My better poems began from unknowing. Several were ekphrastic, invoking paintings by Andrew Wyeth and Gustave Caillebotte as well as artists' renderings of Maine coastline, Louisiana bayous, and the urban physiognomy of St. Louis. As an experiment, I imagined I was a museum curator, organizing a gallery of poems from those my friends deemed to be the strongest.

I chose a long poem "Louisiana Requiem" that, as a landscape painting, could introduce a gallery exhibition, announcing a theme. This poem features a family's ancestral birth-and-deathbed in Baton Rouge where both processes are occurring almost simultaneously against the backdrop of white supremacy and the murder of innocents. If that "landscape painting," set in the Deep South, were to begin the series, then a triple sonnet, set on the rocky coast of Maine, seemed a way to conclude it. I slid this poem, "Shorelines," into the omega position. Like "Louisiana Requiem," it conflates landscape and body. It mixes an ocean bed with a lovers' bed, and a female speaker tests her experience—of laying claim to her desire— against adages of New England Transcendentalism: truisms so deeply assimilated into American culture that we scarcely recognize them as once revolutionary ideals.

Could a woman living through the disorders of the twenty-first century make use of notions of self-trust, innate divinity in human beings, and nature as a mirror for the soul? And what if the chosen drama of a woman's adult life was not marriage and motherhood, the acquisition of profession and property, but the birth of her artistic self? Could "mothering," as an energy opposed to the death drive, provide an ethic for the survival of our species, our earth?

My book, *Parturition*, mulls these questions. As in a gallery of paintings, arranged loosely around a network of themes, each poem presents a different take. Thinking of poems in this way allowed me to revise them toward surprising places, startling honesties. I wrote poems about loving women and men. I wrote about an older friend's escape from sexual exploitation into a career at a prestigious medical school. I wrote about a childhood survivor of the Holocaust who was both her teacher and mine. I extrapolated from what these friends had shared about what they had learned, how they had survived. I thought about the conscious construction of self in a country premised on ahistoricity, of being able to invent oneself as, F. Scott Fitzgerald writes, "an unbroken series of successful gestures," and how self-invention can be circumscribed by class, race, gender, and ability (2).

I considered the ways in which becoming "self-made" can involve certain kinds of amnesia, a willingness to overlook contradictions. I thought about my own contradictions and how lives can skate narrowly above (or be torn apart by) paradox. I wrote about a brilliant literary theorist who teetered, while I knew her, on the knife-edge of life-threatening anorexia as her professional authority grew. I wrote of the middle-class American phenomenon of watching the nightly news—the nightmares of children in cages and rafts—before retiring to the safe harbor of one's bed. In the collection's titling poem, "Parturition," the clinical term for childbirth, a female speaker recalls a brief interval in which she considered the possibility of having or adopting a child, a yearning that turns out to be a "ghostly infatuation" not, as cultural narratives suppose, a mandate of a biological clock (10). In this poem, I drew on conversations with friends, colleagues, and perfect strangers who admitted to being ambivalent parents, who recounted frightening erasures of selfhood in the sheer labor of maternity (or paternity) in a country that offers little support for working families.

I was interested in how personal sacrifices are often hidden in a froth of Hallmark platitudes and normative pressure. In the poem, I compare working mothers to male Athenian citizens in antiquity, conscripted into rowing triremes, or triple-tiered warships, into nautical battle. At what point does service become self-annihilation? Was it possible to "win the war" of having a career and children, for example, but lose the battle for an authentic self?

Next to longer discursive poems, I placed shorter ones, keeping Horace's advice about modulation in mind. A very brief poem, "Nullipara," takes the clinical term for a woman of child-bearing age who has no children, and reclaims it as a category of worth rather than lack:

> Since fruit trees, medlars and mulberries,
> aren't the only arbors required
> to sustain life as we have known it:
> cherish more than your ravenous mouth. (12)

Thinking about whose desire is judged desirable, and what desires are thought "good" or "profligate" and "selfish," I was unearthing not just my frustration with the narrowness of these cultural ideals but also, I hoped, the poverty that comes from abiding by them.

VI. Our Looks, Two Looks

Parturition had no answers to its central questions, only angles of perception arranged in a petite gallery of images and sounds. One of the models I had in mind for a small book was Elizabeth Bishop's *Geography*

III (1976). That collection, though just ten poems, cemented her permanence in American letters. It begins in her birthplace of Worcester, Massachusetts, with a six-year-old child wondering, in a dentist's waiting room,
"what it was I was," while she scarcely dares to look *up* at the adults around
her (6). And the book concludes with the poem "Five Flights Up," in which
an adult narrator cannot help but look *down* from an apartment building,
at daybreak, and envy a "little black dog" romping in the fall leaves, obliv-
ious to reprimand (49).

The whole book, in fact, plays with perspective, in the Latinate sense
of *looking through*. Her narrators peer up and down, gaze from a plane
over a city and a bus in rural Nova Scotia. In "12 O' Clock News," her
speaker views televised images of a foreign war from his or her well-
appointed living room, the antiseptic rhetoric of the broadcast unable to
disguise warfare's ghastliness (32–35). In another poem, her speaker studies
a relative's painting of a familiar place, noting "Our visions coincided"
(38). Art has allowed poet and painter to see the same scene.

As I assembled *Parturition*, I kept in mind how Bishop curated her
collection around these visual dynamics as well as recurrent concerns: the
ethical responsibilities of a North American white woman born into
privilege; the condition of Joycean exile from one's country of birth; the
elegiac recuperation of loss; and the worth of art and the "little we get for
free" in a mass market economy (38). I thought about the many directions
in which she asks her reader to look and how varying distances from her
poems' subjects create, as Horace suggested, a counter-rhythm alongside
narrative congruence or counterpoint. Dramatizing this dynamic, John
Berryman suggests that "you lead the reader in one direction, then you
spin him around, or you sing him a lullaby and then you hit him on the
head" (xviii). Surprise need not be as concussive as Berryman writes, but
shifts in perspective are a key element in assembling a book that invites
the reader in closer and then asks him or her to take a step back and look
again, differently.

"Get obsessed and stay obsessed," my collegiate mentor Michael Harper
said, a clause that always made me think of Claude Monet's series of backlit
haystacks, those gorgeous dumplings of grass that, despite their modest
subject, teach us something about the chimerical qualities of light. Or

Georgia O'Keeffe's surprisingly sensual series of cattle bones, picked clean by vultures, wind, and weather. My first book had taken me twenty years to write. To be able to write. An artist holds a grudge against the gravitational laws that govern a particular historical reality. But in finding a language in which to score that resistance, we locate—to borrow from Seamus Heaney—"images and symbols adequate to our predicament" (56). Working on poems as if they were paintings, I had something I was not reluctant to hang on the wall beside my name and hat.

VII. Epistle

One's family name is the first inheritance, the first tradition or thing handed down. My father had left teaching the same year in which I began kindergarten, and he set up his "office desk," or half a church pew stretched across two file cabinets, in the corner of my bedroom. These two events were linked in my four-year-old mind: my father's retreat from the classroom and my entry into it. He would soon find success in business, coaching Olympic-level runners, but it was up to me to achieve something in the arena he had left behind. The books in his library became mine to investigate. It was my job, I thought, to put our family name on that shelf since my father had left teaching to send me to the best school he could afford.

Joyce's Gabriel Conroy is also a dedicated teacher, one who prides himself on being "right as the mail" or as reliable as the postman in delivering the personal news of letters and, figuratively, the news of literature (201). In the decades since I sat in my father's classroom, a Lilliput at his large desk, I have wondered if he chose to teach that story and to read Conroy's final monologue as a way of telling his students how he felt about leaving them, and his beloved profession, after ten years. I have also wondered if Conroy's speech, in which he retreats to the redoubt of language to acknowledge what he cannot know, was also a letter in a bottle, a belated epistle from my father. At midlife, Conroy grapples with the complexity of those whom he loves, the contradictory country in which he lives, and the disrupted certainties he had felt in being "right as the mail" and "male" of his household.

Like my father, like Conroy, I became a literature teacher, and the allowance for unknowing that Conroy discovers has become essential to both how I teach and write. At the denouement of Joyce's story, Conroy wishes that he was a painter in a blush of yearning for his wife, Gretta, whom he sees atop a staircase as if for the first time:

> There was grace and mystery in her attitude as if she were a symbol of something. He asked himself what is a woman standing on the stairs in the shadow, listening to distant music, a symbol of. If he were a painter he would paint her in that attitude.....*Distant Music* he would call the picture if he were a painter. (240)

Conroy creates a portrait of Gretta, even giving it a title. He paints language on the canvas of memory to preserve the moment. Yet as he finds out later that night, Gretta has been moved by a song that recalled an early love, a tenor who died young, and she seems more enraptured by elegiac feeling for him than she does by her husband and settled life. What Conroy is left with, upon this shattering discovery, is the cold solace of language with which he can cloak—like the snow, general all over Ireland—the hard lines of his revelation.

Was my father telling me that language is what we have, in moments that might otherwise defeat clear understanding? Was he painting me a version of himself through Joyce's story, or suggesting that I, too, would search for images and symbols adequate to experience? Most days, I sit at a wooden desk where my feet now touch the floor, and the light falls through my study's window. I have not lost the shyness that often makes me consider, for a moment, the variety of people's shoes. But I have begun to find a way of depicting—or painting in words—what it is I see or imagine with the hope that my "look" might lend recognizable shape, color, or detail to the landscape in which the reader might also find herself, looking.

Works Cited

Berryman, John. *Collected Poems, 1937–1971*, edited by Charles Thornbury. Farrar Straus Giroux, 1989.

Bidart, Frank. *Half-Light, Collected Poems 1965–2016*. Farrar Straus Giroux, 2017.

Bishop, Elizabeth. *Geography III*. Farrar Straus Giroux, 1976.

Bollas, Christopher. "The Aesthetic Moment and the Search for Transformation." *The Annual of Psychoanalysis*, vol. 6, 1978, pp. 385–394.

Dickinson, Emily. *Complete Poems*, edited by Thomas H. Johnson. Little, Brown and Company, 1960.

———. *Selected Letters*, edited by Thomas H. Johnson. Belknap Press, 1971.

Eliot, T. S. *The Complete Poems and Plays, 1909–1950*. Harcourt Brace, 1980.

Fitzgerald, F. Scott. *The Great Gatsby*. Charles Scribner's Sons, 1953.

Frost, Robert. *The Letters of Robert Frost to Louis Untermeyer*. Holt Rinehart, 1963.

Heaney, Seamus. "Feeling into Words," *Preoccupations, Selected Prose 1968–1978*. Faber and Faber, 1980.

Horace, *The Collected Works of Horace*. trans. Lord Dunsany and Michael Oakley. J. M. Dent, 1960.

Joyce, James. "The Dead," *Dubliners*. Knopf, 1991.

Larrabee, S. "ut pictura poesis," *The Princeton Encyclopedia of Poetry and Poetics*, edited by Alex Preminger. Princeton University Press, 1974.

Scarry, Elaine. *On Beauty and Being Just*. Princeton University Press, 1999.

Treseler, Heather. *Parturition*. Southword Editions, 2020

FAQ

from Press Authors, Graduate Students, and Editing Clients

Christopher Salerno

I've written dozens of poems—do I have a book?

IF YOU ARE friends with poets on social media, you may have scrolled past a familiar image from time to time: the layout shot. Sixty-plus 8.5 x 11 sheets laid out across a hardwood floor or hung up with clothespins, strung like bunting along hastily tied twine (my preferred method). You need this tactile and visual experience with your drafts if you are to become mindful about their potential as a collection. The moment of spontaneous overflow having passed, this is the period of tranquility in which you hope to make something larger out of your individual poems. For this stage you will need other parts of your brain and a lot of space to lay the poems out. It's important to take the wide view, to see the poems together from a distance. Hang your poems along the wall one by one, the way they would pictures in an art gallery. Get them at eye level and stare into them. You need to be able to zoom in on one poem while, using your peripheral vision, you measure it against the surrounding poems. Are the poems familial? Do they speak to each other? Try the poems out in a different order. They will begin to group up, to form cliques, and to show their complementary colors. Now look for resonant connections, obvious themes, similar DNA, likeminded questions raised and questions answered: locate their tones; gather all poems set in similar seasons, poems that travel to the same locales or those you think would best begin or end a section or even the whole book. But don't presume right away that these likeminded poems must necessarily go right beside each other. When collecting and arranging poems in a manuscript, weaving is a better metaphor than stacking. Do this well and the book as a whole will succeed at transcending its individual poems and come to life as a larger presence.

Does my book of poems need a narrative chronology like a book of prose?

As poetry people, there is a bit of projection we do (from more narrative genres) when we talk about books of poems. *Book* is such a loaded word. It comes with expectations of narrative, chronology, and story, and the expectation that the reader is going to have a reliably linear experience. A book of poems need not have a chronological or linear narrative but, absent that, there probably ought to be some aspects of the book that showcase a progression or evolution. This is a question of genre conventions. A few hours after I've finished reading a book of poems, the book takes the form a large meteor shower in my mind. If you've ever watched the Leonid meteor shower, your general impression is that the entire sky is dancing above you, and yet your eyes can only really watch one flitting meteor at a time. And then the next. And then the next. A day later, I am left with a general impression of smaller movements as well as the larger impression of the sky as a whole.

As a kid, I remember being obsessed with "choose your own adventure books"—paperbacks that invite you to select the path the narrative will go by skipping to this or that section in the book. A poetry book, like a "choose your own adventure," can offer a dynamic and multidimensional narrative, which may be why it feels perfectly fine to pick up a book of poems, let it fall open to a random page, read something delightful, flip to another page and do it again. You can move to the middle or the end of the book and still there is some satisfaction and cohesion because each poem will offer its own beginning and end. Each poem along the way declares its own independence while hopefully serving the book's greater good. That said, there are clever and brilliant ways to showcase growth, evolution, epiphany, or emergence by the end of a book of poems, and you would do well to look for them as you put the book together.

How do I go about ordering the poems in my book?

There's a reason we sometimes refer to poetry books as "collections" of poems. Once determined to create a manuscript of poems, some poets find they are rifling through their desk, opening this drawer and that, finding loose or lost poems here and there for the great "collection." But we aren't writing a "collected" or "selected" poems here, as those are special occasions in the genre. For us, there is much to consider when ordering and placing poems. As human beings, we grow up with story and a narrative arc. We have Freytag's dramatic "Pyramid" tattooed on our bones. But as poets we are likely more at ease attending to one poem on one page at a time, teasing out each small arc. To go about ordering, we need to lay out the poems and start trying them in different incarnations.

Strategies for ordering include identifying, gathering, and grouping poems together and then weaving them until you sense that you are building toward a demonstration of growth, evolution, catharsis, reconciliation, or something resonant that moves us from one place to another. What does it mean to be "moved"? Do you want this for your reader? If so, you need to take us somewhere by the end that is different from where we began. Once you have a tentative layout, consider how your particular fixations or obsessions are playing out now that the poems are rubbing elbows. You will likely want to revise certain poems based on redundancies of image, staleness or redundancy of tone, length and breadth of poems as it pertains to the overall pacing, and then assess them for their overall thematic strengths. You will spend a considerable amount of time auditioning poems for prominent slots in the manuscript. As you do this, remember that simply linking poems by titles or last lines/first lines is clever, but not sufficient as the main binding agent for a book. An echo or ping of a word or image is not the same as thematic, mythological, narrative continuity or connection.

What if I just keep writing random poems and see what I end up with later?

Whether you consult your compass or simply follow the sun, both approaches can lead you to a good book. Emily Dickinson and Walt Whitman, the grandparents of modern American poetry, could not have been more different in their style and approach. We think of Dickinson, writing poem and scrap after poem and scrap, and placing each one in the drawer for later. Meanwhile, hundreds of miles away, Whitman was refining and adding to the same collection over and over, letting his great book reel and run like a big fish. We know that he added to and revised the same manuscript throughout his life, right up to his death. And we assume that Dickinson was less concerned with her poems as a bound collection. I would argue that these two approaches landed their respective poets in roughly the same place in the end, like a photo finish of the tortoise and the hare.

Whether you can allow yourself to write poem after poem without knowing where you're headed probably depends on your personality and experience. I, for one, find it difficult, after writing even a dozen new poems, not to get meta about what I'm "doing." I like to know where I'm going so that I can condition myself to capture any ideas I may have during my waking hours. I also know that I've written books of both kinds, and I now prefer the process of writing with an eye on one dominant idea or theme. But I'm not forceful. Not a day goes by when a poet hasn't chimed in on another poet's anecdote about this or that plight to say, "There's a poem in there!" Personally, I smile and agree, but I never write the poem. To try would be a waste of time for me, since poems are, after all, mostly out of my control. But when writing toward a book of poems, I *can* continue to throw objects in my own path and hope for the best.

I've seen many manuscripts written by poets who didn't follow a compass, and they were just as likely to be great and compelling books. It's important to point out that you are a unique person using language in a way that honors and propels your idiosyncrasies and obsessions—there is likely going to be some level of consistency across your poems. As an editor and manuscript consultant, I've also seen a lot of manuscripts-in-progress that felt like a series of little projects strung together, thus creating a number of wells or compartments in the book. A section on travel poems here, a section of prose poems there, a section of poems about the death of a loved one, followed by a series of ekphrastic poems. While it might prove difficult to put all of this in a book that feels cohesive, the good news is that, by writing these suites of likeminded poems, you might be investing in future projects.

What if I don't know whether my book is ABOUT something?

What does about mean? Personally, I find words such as about and meaning to be suspect. And especially in the context of writing a book of poems. Forcing meaning in poetry is like trying to force healing. Healing never happens in a straight line. Now, if your book happens to show readers the crooked path of healing, then I'd say your book is about healing. Likewise, we know there are no straight lines in nature (ok, pyrite, I see you, but let me finish). My argument is that once you've written a book of poems, it is by default about something because (a) it is full of words arranged in a deliberate order and (b) it is nearly impossible to write sixty pages of poetry without the emergence of some overarching personality, and (c) you are a human who has lived for thousands of days. Once you rub two poems together you have narrative, you have story. However, the reality of publishing suggests that a poetry book requires some justification for its publication. Try reading the catalogue copy for your favorite poetry distributor, and then see whether you can write a three-hundred-word description of your own book. Begin it with the phrase, "In so-and-so's debut collection...." Force yourself to reach the three-hundred words.

Maybe your book doesn't need to rationally or logically be about something, but rather it may be a demonstration of a particular frequency, an energy, or an expression of a heightened state of mind. Dorothea Lasky, a wildly original poet, once wrote, "Poetry Is Not a Project," an essay calling poets back from the brink of the mediocrity one can fall into when forcing "projects" upon themselves. "Just because you have constructed a project does not mean you have written a poem," Lasky says. You can plan a party, but you have to make the people show up for it to really be a party" (25).

Some poets do best to follow their own impulses and instincts rather than a defined project. In *The Birth of Tragedy*, Friedrich Nietzsche designates two dominant forces that we can also use to consider poetic manner and style: "Apollonian" and "Dionysian." One might say all types of form or structure and rational thought are inherently Apollonian. On the other hand, the Dionysian is characterized by enthusiasm and ecstasy. Apollonian versus Dionysian impulses appear across the board when surveying poetry manuscripts. In the social media era, highly expressive lyric poets working in some of the more voice-driven modes eschew elements like conventional punctuation and capitalization. Their books, aside from their obvious content or what they are about, can easily lean on style to build cohesion and consistency. Carmen Giménez Smith's *Be Recorder* is one of the most various, dynamic books of poems I've read in the previous few years. Various and overflowing, it dashes between tight poems, long poems, prose poems, poems arranged by field, poems with dramatic white space, poems narrow and poems fat. But the voice and the particular brand of Dionysian rebelliousness forms the cohesive sense across the book's varied pages. Contrast that to a poet like Henri Cole or Louise Glück, and you can see how "about" can be expressed through style, form, and manner as well as through content. If I want to get the book published, do I need to write a "Theme" or "Project" Book?

No! Yes! No. Unification across a manuscript of poetry can mean so many things. Maybe the rhetoric across the poems is consistently skittery and associative, or the voice consistently vatic or comic or self-deprecating. Maybe the poems tend to invest in catharsis or climax in an idiosyncratic but consistent way. Maybe a particular brand of surrealism or humor runs through the poems, or the imagery is particularly grounded in a specific and recurring location or place. Publishers seem to agree that there is a threshold at which a book is a "book." I like this quote by Ralph Waldo Emerson: "In this pleasing contrite wood-life which God allows me, let me record day by day my honest thought without prospect or retrospect, and, I cannot doubt it, it will be found symmetrical, though I mean it not and see it not. My book should smell of pines and resound with the hum of insects" (203). You might write a theme book without planning to write a theme book.

I know so many poets who have published every last poem in their manuscript but still it cannot find a home. I see these come through the submission system regularly, and while they feature great poems they may, in the end, solicit remarks from internal reviews such as, "The poems are great, but is there a book here?" A book, then, is a "book" when it offers some level of consistency, whether it be topical, stylistic, formal, or otherwise. Some books are a string of lights and others are a string of lights in a tangled pile in the grass—both can be equally as bright, but a lot of publishers are invested in something they can describe in three-hundred words of catalogue copy.

Does my manuscript have to have sections?

No, but the last thirty books I've edited for publication have had sections. Most of the books I've read have sections. I believe that one or more section breaks across a manuscript with over sixty pages of poetry is often a necessary device to separate smaller thematic arcs, or else it's simply a little gift to a reader to encourage them to slow down. Consider your book as a curator would consider the pieces to be hung on the blank white gallery walls inside a large hall or art gallery. I feel about the same way when moving from one section of a poetry book to another as I do moving from one room to the next in a museum. Has the artist created different series that deserve designated areas? How will the patrons move through the room/manuscript, and what objects will be placed where? Ultimately, I think people are conditioned to read too quickly and may fly through your work at 1.5 times the optimal speed. If they aren't used to reading poetry they will sail through your linebreaks and stanza breaks and plow forward as they do with any other text in order to consume the information. Sections, therefore, can be a gift. Seen another way, you might take the idea of the caesura and apply it in a broader sense to the manuscript as a whole. If you have the opportunity of slowing readers down a little bit, letting the gravity of what they're reading linger for a few more beats, then that's a good move. The Greek idea of *kairos* means taking advantage of or even creating a perfect moment to deliver a particular message. When considering the arrangement of sections (and even the ordering of poems), kairos comes into play.

How many sections are too many for a book of poetry? I don't suggest using more than three, and I believe you should be able to justify why three sections are necessary for the book. Absent some brilliant and mindful thematic structure, beware the instinct to create more than three sections, as this might suggest you are dumping poems in different piles because they don't "go" anywhere else.

Should I include one of those prefatory poems I see in a lot of poetry books?

The prefatory poem, one of your poems placed before the opening of the body of the book (as distinct from an epigraph), is certainly en vogue. I've suggested prefatory poems to people I've worked with over the years, but only because at some point during the editing process I was so struck by what I call a "flagship" poem in a manuscript that I thought it would lend itself well as an introduction to the book's overall mythology while also foregrounding something vital. Or else that particular poem makes an obvious door to book. Usually these poems have a vatic quality, or else carry a good bit of gravitas or large-scale magic. How do I know which poems to put next to which?

Naturally, once we place them in a manuscript, our poems play different roles there than they do on their own. Some poems are natural openers, some are builders, some are bridges, some are closers, some are palette cleansers. We can't fully know this until we begin assembling our book. Some poems that could never find a home in a magazine now serve the book in vital ways because of how they lend context, offer some backstory, or otherwise help hold up the larger project. When it comes to putting together a book, some poems need a little help from their friends. I've described a book of poetry as having areas of what one might call "prime real estate." Highly visible plots of land upon which you will place a structure that will receive a good deal of attention. Some of these prime real estate areas (some optional) include a prefatory poem, opening and closing of each section, title poem, final poem, etc. Once you lay it all out, candidates for these slots will begin to emerge. Another idea is to consider whether a section with repetitive themes or approaches (definition poems, object poems, recipe poems, etc.) makes sense in the manuscript. If I put too many of these poems next to each other, the reader may begin to compare them. However, if I disperse them strategically throughout the manuscript, they have a chance on their own to delight and surprise the reader as well as offer some echoes and connectedness on a larger scale. When you read Morgan Parker's book, *Magical Negro,* you can see seven title poems scattered throughout the book. That, and the numbers, "Magical Negro #217," "Magical Negro #607," etc." give the impression that there are hundreds and hundreds of these numbered title poems, that the mythology behind the book is enormous. This is a brilliant move for the way it creates a broad and believable backstory. Had these poems all been placed in sequential order or set up to comprise one section of the book, these poems would have competed with each other. Instead, they help form the book's connective tissue, build backstory, and bring us back again and again to the book's most powerful themes at several points.

How far is too far to place two poems away from each other if they are intended to speak to each other across the pages? When you think about it, most of the poems in the average poetry manuscript are more like cousins than they are siblings. They didn't grow up in the same house but they are all together now for the High Holiday. Put another way, unless we have a definite progression or chronology to the poems we've written, arranging a book of poetry is more about weaving than it is stacking or piling. In plot-driven genres like film and fiction, we often see foreshadowing, or what might be called *recycling*. You see an image of a vase in act one, and that vase is broken in act two. This can be employed when arranging a book of poetry. Usually this pertains to imagery or diction. As a reader, when I get a ping back to something from a few pages ago, the part of my brain that appreciates the progression of story feels rewarded for having read closely some pages ago. Not the previous page, but perhaps a few pages back. More importantly, this kind of connection or consistency across pages helps build the world of the book. In later stages of the editing process, I find it important to read the manuscript for areas of redundancy of image and diction as well as look for opportunities to strengthen the relationships between poems across pages by placing them at deliberate distance from each other.

So it sounds like you're saying that all my poems need not be "about" the same thing, but maybe they should be in conversation with each other?

At various points in his recent book, *The Tradition*, Jericho Brown places a series of five "Duplex" poems based on the structure of the Ghazal, which is driven by the repetition of lines. The poems speak to each other and to the themes in the book. His use of the form culminates in the final "Duplex: Cento," which combines the major themes and ideas of the collection by directly quoting lines from its various poems. This is a very clever way to bring a collection of poems together while bringing to light the cycle of tradition.

When I read a book of poetry, I am interested in subjectivity, the idiosyncratic nature of a poet's vision of the world. This unique vision and perspective can make a book come together when content-cohesion and narrative arc are absent or less dominant across the book. Similarly, there is a difference between the subject of your poems and the tone of your poems. Tone can bring certain poems into conversation and also help to build a sense of movement and arrival. Many books of poetry are held together by tone, vision, and perspective, since these elements are usually consistent for poets. Sophisticated poets know how to use these to create a dynamic architecture inside of the book.

I'm fascinated by the late Denis Johnson's poetry books and the many exquisite portraits of strangers found therein. These portraits offer no real mythological tie-in to the speaker's lyric arc necessarily, but they offer a distinct tone and a unique perspective on the world, and these poems are therefore in conversation with any other poems by nature of the poet's nature. The idiosyncratic can definitely be enough to foster cohesion. Our poems, once bound together in a collection, will converse with each other in many ways beyond their content.

Is it a problem if I haven't published all the poems in my manuscript?

No, but if you've been trying like mad to publish your poems everywhere and they have been roundly rejected, it could suggest that the individual poems aren't ready. As an editor screening book manuscripts for a contest, I don't spend much time studying acknowledgements pages. And countless books that go on to win contests have as little as a third of their poems published before submission. Some have even less. Yes, it's impressive if you've published many or all of the book's poems in reputable magazines, but this does not mean you necessarily have a well-tuned book on your hands. Personally, when I'm building toward my own book-length manuscripts, I use the magazine submission process (sending batches of individual poems) as a basic kind of validation, but nothing more. Publishing an individual poem lets me feel okay about leaving it alone by itself for a while as I work on others.

I've known many friends and editing clients who have published every poem in their manuscript but still cannot get the book accepted by a press. The book has been a semifinalist here and a finalist there, but it continues to struggle to find a home. Why? Because some other manuscript in the pile had a more compelling book-feel, a more definable arc, or perhaps a more compelling or original voice. This tells me that you ought not be overly concerned with publishing all of the poems in a manuscript before submitting it for publication. And definitely don't count on every publication as assurance that a particular poem doesn't need you anymore. Even published poems want to hear from you again once you've started laying out a manuscript. Don't forget, once your manuscript is ordered and populated, you may want to revise some poems based on their new situation and surroundings. You may have redundancies of image or language that now seem awkward or distracting in the manuscript. Further revision of individual poems happens even after the manuscript has been arranged and ordered.

How does the editing process work when you do have a publisher?

Actual editing of content, form or style varies wildly across the poetry publishing world. In my experience as poet, there is very little developmental "editing" at university presses unless the press has a designated poetry editor. That said, I've had friends who have found themselves questioning why a press accepted their book in the first place since they were asking for so many changes to the book. I've published with university presses who only engaged in copyediting, and I've worked with smaller presses who fully dug in to my manuscript. As an editor myself, I try to offer the full editing experience, which begins with the following set of questions I send to poets early in the process.

Five Questions for the First Pass:

1. I'd like you to describe your book for me in no more than three hundred words. What do you see as the book's central claim? What are you doing here? Why is this a book? Which poems in the manuscript are crucial to making this case? This need not be exclusively a discussion of your book's content/themes. Feel free to discuss style, manner, vision, values, language, identity, or any other element you feel compelled to discuss here in describing your book.

2. Can you describe your book's dominant form, mode, or manner? How do you like to create drama or tension or quiet or concentration on the page with your lines, stanzas, shapes, or white space? Or, how do you see your poems using the *field* of the page? What do you care about in terms of form?

3. What is your rationale for the current ordering and layout and/or sectioning of this manuscript?

4. What, if anything, worries you about the manuscript? Nothing? Great!

5. I'd like you to make two lists (of titles from your manuscript). Your "A-game" poems, and your "B-game" poems. I'm not asking you to spend forever on this, or even to name all of your poems. Just name those poems you KNOW should be in either list.

Your A-Gamers:

A-gamers feel finished to you. They have been published on the face of the moon, or you and everyone you know loves them. Alternatively, you could see these poems as flagships for the book as a whole, or as perfect demonstrations of you as a poet of distinction doing "your thing" right now on the planet. Or else maybe you see them as demonstrations of where you are taking "your thing" with this particular book. In your opinion, there would be no book without these poems.

Your B-Gamers:

If you have any, give me a list of the poems you feel consciously or subconsciously worried about for whatever reason. These would not make the first list. Maybe these were rejected by your favorite journals, or they haven't gotten the attention in revision that they could have, or you don't feel like they are your best work for some reason. These are the poems that, right before giving a reading, you stick back into your notebook and bail on. Maybe you have none? That's okay, too. Let's also assume and expect that any poems in the book play their role in the arc of manuscript, regardless of how "finished" or "rough" you think they are. Placement and arc can change how we think about all of the above.

The Process:

I'm going to read your notes (generated from my questions above) and then read your manuscript and make notes throughout using the Track Changes function in MS Word. Mostly I will try to reflect back what I see happening in your book. Some comments might be about a whole poem, or a section, a beginning or an ending, the order, or any matters of proofreading if I see them. My goal is to help your manuscript *do its thing* more effectively by holding the larger view of the manuscript as I read each poem.

What strategies of deconstruction can you add to your construction?

Every spring I watch the jenny wrens build a new nest in the birdhouse in my yard. Birds the size of my thumb bring one little twig after another to the front hole and then, if one twig is too long to fit inside, the negotiating begins. Often the tiny bird can't carry the twig through the hole without tilting and turning its head, trying it this way and that. Sometimes the twig falls to the ground, at which point the bird has to get a new grip on that particular twig and try again to get it through the hole and add it to the nest. Sometimes, after several attempts, the bird gives up on that twig and goes in search of another one. Eventually, the nest is woven, at which point the bird will use its breast to press against the material, which is how the form of the nest is made. In the fall, when I clean out the box,

I'm always delighted at what little oddities like wrappers, bits of ribbon, or scraps of paper have been woven in.

In French, one word for a rough draft is *brouillon*, meaning "rough, placed in disorder, scrambled." This metaphor, when taken as a framework for a poetry manuscript, suggests a process that begins with disorder. Personally, I like when some of that disorder, some of the tension inherent to forming and shaping a book of various independent pieces, is reflected in the final product. Why? Because a book is most human, most organic, when it carries some record of the poet's process. Because, as Rilke said, "A work of art is good if it has sprung from necessity. In this nature of its origin lies the judgment of it: there is no other." When we go about collecting and arranging our poems into a book, we can't help but allow some disorder into the book, which I believe conveys authenticity.

I remember asking the legendary poet Robert Bly about why he and his contemporaries largely put aside meter and rhyme in the middle of the twentieth century. His answer? "We had become insufficiently ourselves." Historically, we have also seen scores of poets devoted to alternative formalism, such Marianne Moore or Gwendolyn Brooks, two exemplars who recognized form as inherently ideological and set about reimagining it, subverting it, therefore highlighting its otherness. Today, many of the greatest new books of poetry are particularly good at honoring their own disorder, allowing for disruption, incorporating and even showcasing the necessary messes of the urgent lyric moment. These books may be notable for their rebellious manner and style, or they are otherwise less concerned with conventional uses of standard written English. Simply put, they carry an urgency, a need to speak in whatever manner or voice or register is most conducive to making it happen NOW—tradition be damned. I would guess that your favorite contemporary poets are likely to be quite distinct from each other aesthetically. What they will likely have in common, however, is the ability to incorporate, weave into, or amplify their idiosyncrasies across the arc of the book.

Visually, a book of poems, before we begin to read it, is more like a flip book that, when you let its pages fly with your thumb, offers a blur of verse in various forms and lengths, widths of lines cast out or drawn close. And so the overall construction of a poetry book inherently captures and preserves disruption over and over again. A published book of poems contains dramatic amounts of white space, poems with various formal features, half-empty pages, blank pages, sections, lines that wander longingly toward the margin or end abruptly, and yet the through line of the book continues on again and again. Sometimes the poems carry a pattern of unique mannerisms, an eccentric prosody, a consistency of breath or breathlessness in the lines—all of these are elements of the book's construction. On one hand there are rests, ebbs, eddies and eruptions in a book of poetry. On the other hand, the book is a book because of its overarching concerns and consistencies. When these forces combine and complement each other, that's usually when a book turns brilliant.

Works Cited

Bly, Robert. Personal interview. Conducted by Christopher Salerno, June 2003.
Emerson, Ralph W. *Self-Reliance*. Peter Pauper Press, 1967.
Lasky, Dorothea. *Poetry Is Not a Project*. Ugly Duckling, 2010.
Rilke, Rainer Maria. *Letters to a Young Poet*. Penguin Classics, 2016.

The Body of the Poetry Manuscript
Patterning Your Collection with Structural Repetition

Annie Finch

THERE IS A secret to writing poetry, and it's one that has been largely forgotten. I teach poetry writing to people of all levels of expertise and many backgrounds, and most of them arrive at my classes in a state of significant frustration. They love poetry, and they have high expectations for their own poems. Yet, even if they hold an advanced degree in creative writing, they have likely never been taught the tools necessary to create the moving, inspiring, heightened shapes of many of the great poems they know and love—or even how to shape a poem until it feels "finished" to them.

The good news is that this forgotten knowledge hews to an intuitive, accessible principle. Poets in my classes find that the principle, which I call "structural repetition," yields useful guidelines for heightening the language of poems:

1. Notice anything that repeats in your poem: a rhythm, a word-sound, syntax...
2. Reorganize your poem, creating a pattern out of the repeating things.
3. Revise, add, and subtract to heighten your favorite repeating elements.
4. Consider allowing some repetitions to become predictable.

Much else that can be learned about structuring poems—line, meter, scansion, stanza, form—develops from here. Basic enough—but life-changing, for those of us who have not been conscious of the single defining characteristic of the art we love. Since the early twentieth century, the academy's focus on the page has led to a general overlooking of the uniquely palpable experience of poetic structure in the body. With that physical awareness at heart, I start with the premise that structural language patterning (pattern created through the structural repetition of any language element or elements) is the single defining characteristic of poetry.

This doesn't mean that only poetry uses patterned, repeating language. Prose can also use gorgeous, lyrical, repetitive, incantatory language patterning. But while prose can be decorated by pattern, only poems are structured by pattern. A structuring pattern is predictable, reliable; if it were a wall, it would be a load-bearing wall. If a structural pattern stops, the reader will perceive that something is broken and will know how it should be fixed, just the way someone who sees a hole in fabric or a crack in a clay pot will know it is broken and how it should be fixed.

Here is a passage of prose and a passage of poetry by the same author, James Joyce. In each example, I have changed one of the repeating words. In the poetry, the consequences are structural, while in the prose, they are not.

> …and Gibraltar as a girl where I was a Flower of the mountain yes when I put the rose in my hair like the Andalusian girls used or shall I wear a red yes and how he kissed me under the Moorish wall and I thought well as well him as another and then I asked him with my eyes to ask again yes and then he asked me would I yes to say yes my mountain flower and first I put my arms around him yes and drew him down to me so he could feel my breasts all perfume sweet and his heart was going like mad and yes I said yes I will Yes. (*Ulysses* 732–33)

> Frail the white rose, and frail are
> Her hands that gave,
> Whose soul is sere, and paler
> Than time's wan wave.
>
> Rose-fair and fair, yet frailest—
> A wonder wild,
> In gentle eyes thou veilest,
> My blue-veined sweet. (*Collected Poems* 40)

In the original version of the first passage, the repeating word ("yes") appears ten times—and yet readers who don't know the passage won't perceive that I changed one "yes" to the word "sweet"; if anyone does notice, they will respond to the change as a matter of taste and aesthetics, not structural necessity. By contrast, in the original version of the second passage, the second repeating sound ("ild") only appears twice—and yet attentive readers who don't know the passage will notice that I changed one of these appearances to the word "sweet." They will know something is broken, and they will know how to fix it—by replacing the word "sweet" with a word that rhymes with "wild." The repetitions of "yes" create no predictable structural pattern; they are decorative. The repetitions of "ild" creates a predictable pattern; they are structural. This is the difference between decorative and structural repetition in language.

This difference has nothing to do with aesthetic quality. It is objective, like saying that soup is mostly water and bread mostly flour, that paintings are two-dimensional and sculptures three-dimensional. Some poetry is flat, dull, full of ordinary language, has no decorative repetition, and sounds ugly. But it is still poetry. Some prose is musical, inspiring, loaded with decorative repetition, and sounds gorgeous. But it is still prose. Poetry is made using structural repetition, and prose is not. That's the difference. Sure, there exist exceptions, hybrids, or gray areas—like bread soup, combine paintings, and prose poems—but they don't invalidate the usefulness of a common-sense distinction: structural repetition is the single basic difference between poetry and prose.

Structural repetition can operate at any level of poetry in English: at the level of syllable (structures of syllable count); the level of accent (structures of accent count); the level of word-music (such as alliteration, consonance, and rhyme); the level of word (where words repeat exactly, such as identical rhyme or the repetends in a sestina); the level of concept (structures such as S +7); the level of visual effect (repeating effects with visual impact such as concrete poetry or erasure poetry); the level of metrical foot (anapestic, iambic, trochaic, dactylic, amphibrachic, etc.); the level of phrase (including anaphora and refrain); the level of syntax (such as parallelism or repeating parts of speech); the level of line (the structural repetition of the line break itself, which marks free verse as poetry); the level of metrical line (sapphic, hendecasyllabic, etc.); the level of stanza (structures of rhyme, repetition, rhetoric, and so on); the level of length (the acceptable length before the ending which seems to mark a prose poem as a poem); the level of form (ghazal, haiku, pantoum, sonnet, villanelle, etc.); and the level of the book.

When structural repetition is applied at the level of the book, an overarching repeating structure generates a series of sections that can organize a multifarious collection of disparate poems into a movingly cohesive manuscript. This higher-level organizing element—I call it an organizing structural principle (OSP)—not only brings the sections into relation with each other, but also brings each poem into relation with its own subsection and in turn into relation with the organizing structural principle.

Samuel Coleridge wrote that all parts of a work of art should connect with all other parts, a state he called "organic unity" (400). If we consider the book of poetry as a work of art, at least three levels of organization are needed to attain the harmonious dance of interrelated parts that Coleridge describes: a whole (the entire manuscript, in the case of a poetry manuscript); individual units of the whole (poems, in the case of a poetry manuscript); and intermediate parts of the whole (sections, in the case of a collection of thematically disparate poems—although in a concept-centered book, such as George Herbert's *The Temple*, Anne Sexton's *Transformations*, Rita Dove's *Thomas and Beulah*, Cathy Bosman's *Letters From Sylvia*, or A. Van Jordan's *M-A-C-N-O-L-I-A* that limit themselves thematically to a single image, context, or narrative, the theme itself can play this role).

These three levels can be arranged in a one-dimensional way, called *parataxis* in syntax: the mid-level clauses are strung together with coordinating conjunctions ("this happened and this happened and this happened and this happened"). A paratactical organization of a book of poetry groups poems into sections based on theme or topic and give those sections numbers or names, arranging one thing next to another thing next to another thing, all at the same level, so that the three levels of the book move more or less in parallel with each other.

By contrast, using an Organizing Structural Principle or OSP creates a more complex type of structure for the manuscript. The grammatical corollary to this type of organization is called *hypotaxis*. In hypotaxis, instead of coordinating conjunctions stringing items along at the same level, subordinating conjunctions link the different clauses into relationships that gain meaning from the level of the whole, creating an interdependent web of all three levels together ("this happened to the words in spite of the fact that this happened to the clauses; therefore, this happened to the sentence"). When you assemble a book of poetry in this way, your aesthetic attention to the links between and among different segments of the book—the synergy and symmetry among parts—can create a poetic impact analogous to, but perhaps even more far-reaching than, the effect of an individual poem.

The witch, writer, and permaculturalist Starhawk speaks about a group of basic natural patterns that are found in paleolithic and neolithic Goddess art—and in contemporary permaculture gardens. One of these perennial natural patterns, the branching tree, offers a useful way to think about hypotactic structure in a book of poems. If the whole book is like the trunk, and the individual poems are like leaves, then the sections that keep everything unified and vibrant are like the branches of the tree. And just as the branches of a tree need to arise organically from the trunk in order to do their job of communicating life and energy back and forth between leaves and trunk, so the parts of an organizing structural principle need to arise organically from an overarching shape, form, or concept that informs the book, if they are going to work effectively to make your manuscript as tensile and unique as a living thing.

The poetic effect of a book that's organized according to a structural principle doesn't only come from the power of the poems themselves; it arises from the manifestation of the poetic sensibility that has arranged disparate poems together with attention to structural repetition. A book interwoven through an OSP is more likely to be felt as a conversation: questions asked by the book as a whole are answered by individual poems; adjacent and analogous sections comment on each other; remarks made by poems or sections are responded to by the book as a whole. The sublime, universal creative process underlying this organizational matrix—a web of connections inviting patterns of love and meaning, both within the book and between book and reader—is the discovery and nurturing of pattern.

The organizing structural principle that will hold together your manuscript can use any form as a model—anything that combines parts into a whole. In my experience, the more disparate the different poems in your manuscript, the stronger and more cohesive the OSP will need to be. Poets who consult with me have discovered all kinds of principles waiting in their poems, ready to help organize the book: a series of compositional modes from music, different members of a family unit, characters in a Shakespeare play, levels of Buddhist meditation. The only requirement for an OSP is that it be as strong and flexible as needed to do its job, both whole and parts holding the inherent structural integrity to interconnect the different poems in your book in a meaningful way.

Principles of structural repetition can operate in how we choose which poems to include in a book, which sections to divide the book into, what to name the sections, how to order the poems within sections, and so on. From William Blake's *Songs of Innocence and Experience* to W. B. Yeats's *The Tower* to Gwendolyn Brooks's *Annie Allen*, poetry collections have been shaped according to the same principles of structure and symmetry that shape poems. My own awareness of this overarching aspect of poetic structure began with my own books. Each of my collections of poems went through an astonishingly long gestation before its final structure emerged. And in each case, only the discovery of the right organizing structural principle broke the impasse.

In 1993, as an assistant professor living in the fields of Northern Iowa with my husband Glen and four-year-old child Julian, I was working on my second book of poetry. I recall it had had several paratactical structures by then, with a new title for each. My first book *The Encyclopedia of Scotland* had been a book-length poem with its own internal structure, so this second book was actually my first poetry collection. And first collections of poetry are notoriously challenging to organize, often including a miscellany of poems written over a long period. The earliest poems in mine, including "Still Life," "Sapphics for Patience," "In Cities, Be Alert," "Coy Mistress," and "Another Reluctance," had been written fifteen years earlier as assignments for undergraduate classes; the latest, a nine-poem sequence about different Goddesses created for a theater collaboration, was brand new and had just premiered at the Hearst Center for Performing Arts under the title "The Furious Sun in Her Mane." The book felt like a hodge-podge. It had been years, and I felt as stumped as ever. How could I possibly unite all this in a meaningful way?

One night after Julian was asleep I sat on the living room floor (since childhood, I have always worked on the floor when organizing anything) and again divided the individual lyric poems into piles based on theme—nature, motherhood, sex, power, spirituality—as I had done many times. I was shuffling through the piles again, as if that would help, when my husband Glen came in from washing the dishes and sat down on the couch.

"How's it going?"

"Not great. I'm really stuck. Hey, can I ask your advice?"

"Sure."

"I want to include the 'Furious Sun in Her Mane' sequence. But it's so different from everything else in the book. I don't know whether to put it at the end of the book or the beginning—they both feel kind of weird. Which do you think would be better?"

"Well, you could break it up—and put one of those poems into each section..."

"Cool. Thanks. I'll try it!"

I had never imagined separating the nine poems in "The Furious Sun in Her Mane," since I had written them as a group. But the idea was perfect. Each of the nine Goddesses I had chosen for my show had Her own mood and Her own powers, from youthful Rhiannon to transformative Inanna—and their characteristics meshed uncannily with the concerns of my earlier poems! To house each Goddess in one of the piles on the floor was a gratifyingly smooth process; only a few sections needed to be combined or rethought. It was uncanny to discover that my earlier poetry dealt with the exact same themes that had shaped my recent poetry/dance collaboration. Not only did it give me a new awareness of myself as an artist with sustaining concerns, it also surprised me spiritually. Before I knew these Goddesses existed, I had been interacting with them simply by engaging with my life as a woman through my poems.

Using the Goddess sequence as an OSP transformed the paratactic arrangement of the book, which I had been messing around with unsuccessfully for years, into a hypotactic arrangement. The new structure situated each poem more exactly in relation to every other poem, both in its own section and beyond, highlighting and deepening the book's themes. And while it more clearly defined and separated the different sections, it also united them, because the Goddess poems connected with each other in multiple ways. Each of the nine poems is named after a Goddess and focuses on evoking and describing her; each one uses a meter and form that would have been used in the culture where its Goddess arose; and the order of the poems, as I had developed it for the dance collaboration, connects all nine into a narrative of spiritual development. While not every OSP needs to have such strong similarities and links between its sub-parts, I find that these connections enhance the value of the structure, both for me as a poet and for the reader absorbing the book.

Incorporating an organizing structural principle into a manuscript can be a beginning as much as an end. Working with an OSP offers me the same feeling—the deep company of limits—that I tend to prefer when composing poems. I am a forceful reviser, and poems without a sturdy skeletal structure for me to work against have sometimes nearly disappeared during revision. Conversely, when I have found or developed a structure that suits me, my poems and books tend to become more themselves, more visible. In this case, after settling on the OSP, I needed to reconsider which poems were included in each section and their order, which deepened and enhanced my understanding of each poem and led in turn to many revisions. I took a new title from one of the Goddess poems and was well on my way into the final stages of the book now called *Eve*.

Paul Valéry wrote, "a poet's function is not to experience the poetic state; that is a private affair. His [sic] function is to create it in others" (62). I love to write in meter and form not only because they often hypnotize me into a "poetic state," but also because I believe their patterns (especially when read aloud) meet readers halfway, pointing the way for readers to recreate the "poetic state" within themselves. And organizing structural principles strike me as useful in precisely the same way. They structure the poetic experience like design in a tapestry, offering readers a chance to experience physically and tangibly the whole, the parts, and the understanding that links the whole and the parts—almost like giving them the experience of recreating the book within themselves. By offering readers this key, I was not only clarifying for them the mood of each section, freeing up more of their energy to experience the poems, but also making the hidden overall "plot" of the book much clearer to those who had not lived with my poetry for years, as I had.

Eve was born in 1997, and my strategy of shaping my poetry collections as if they were poems was launched. Now I revise and work and consider an OSP in basically the same way that I revise and work and consider the structure of a poem. Finishing my next collection, *Calendars*, five years later, I was encouraged by advice from the poet Carolyn Kizer to foreground a group of seven seasonal chants that I had written for an earth-spirituality witches' circle. Again I organized a collection into sections; each section of the book centers on a different part of the year, and metaphorically the seasons also become the seasons of our lives.

My newest poetry collection, *Coven*, completed just recently, is also organized around a sequence of poems, a series of chants to the five directions. It is the most tightly patterned of all my books, since the poems of each section are connected to each other not only by theme but also by the poems' meter, the titles' meter, and even by patterns of punctuation. Thus, the title refers not to any one element but to the shape and movement of the entire book.

Organizing structural principles have been helpful not only for my own books of poems, but also those of many poets who have worked on books with me individually or in classes. Wilderness Sarchild's first collection of poems demonstrates well the usefulness of an organizing structural principle for one of my student's books. At the age of seventy-five, Wilderness brought me a captivating manuscript of assorted poems on the theme of being an older woman. The patterns in the book were based on theme and voice, with some poems that told anecdotes, others that ranted, others that yearned. A parasyntactic approach would have been simply to arrange these charming, readable poems into thematically related groups and call the book done.

But Wilderness's manuscript was so wide and encompassing that I felt it was demanding a more developed structure. I tend to believe there are no coincidences in poetry, so I took this feeling as valid information and stayed alert for a clue, an anomaly that would stand out and lead us in a new direction as we worked to bring the book into its own. And sure enough, among the poems was one that didn't fit properly into any of the sections suggested by the other poems. It was called "Old Women Talking," and it distinguished itself from the other poems not only for its humor and charm—many of the others were humorous and charming as well— but for its length, ambition, and breadth of vision. "Old Women Talking" was an *ars poetica*, a manifesto that perfectly summed up all the themes of the book as a whole.

So we decided to name the book *Old Women Talking*. We put that poem at the beginning of the whole book like a foreword—a sort of map of the whole. Then we arranged the other poems into thematic sections and gave each section a name based on the kinds of talking listed in "Old Women Talking," including Gossiping, Keening, Remembering, Scolding... In the resulting branching structure, each poem gains additional impact and context based on which section it is in and on the relation of that section to the other sections in the book—as well as the relation of those sections to the title poem itself.

To summarize the process I used with Wilderness—which is the process I now use with most of the books of poetry I work on (not all, because there are always exceptions!)—it has three parts:

1. Notice patterns (in Wilderness's case, noticing the various voices threading through the poems).
2. Use the patterns you've noticed to help you discover and choose a structure (in Wilderness's case, choosing the title poem and naming the manuscript).
3. Develop your chosen structure further, to make its pattern(s) more evident to yourself and the reader (in Wilderness's case, adding the section titles).

This process may seem simple in retrospect, yet it is surprising how few contemporary poetry books that would clearly be strengthened by a hypotactic arrangement have made the leap. Aside from the fact that many people simply haven't been taught to think about poetry collections in terms of OSPs, why don't more poets do this?

One reason may be that most of us were taught to write free verse, linking lines along a single plane with the line breaks functioning like "ands" in a paratactic sentence (line and line and line and line and line). When free verse uses repeating device such as parallelism or anaphora, it is usually in a decorative way rather than a structural way: the repetitions are unpredictable, and a reader couldn't tell if the patterns were broken. So we are not in the habit of using structural repetition at the level of the poem, and if we don't use it at the level of the poem it may not occur to us to use it at the level of the book. The truth is, though, that as Wilderness's wonderful free verse collection *Old Women Talking* and the books of many other free verse poets who have worked with me prove, free verse collections can be magnificently organized with OSPs.

Another reason poets may not use OSPs is because we may fear that the use of such a complex structure on the poet's part would be an imposition. Trained by modernism and postmodernism to honor a reader's freedom to create their own interpretative patterns and meanings out of the juxtapositions of words, let alone the juxtaposition of poems, we may find it unseemly and intrusive, even clumsy and annoying, to arrange poems into an obviously intentional structure. This is of course an aesthetic choice that deserves complete respect—obviously, OSPs will not be for everyone!

I will add, though, that having read more than my share of postmodern theory, I find the fears that may accompany such a choice unnecessary. Our interpretative freedom is our interpretative freedom, and no mere poetic structure can undermine it. If anything, I have found that the more a poet can do to develop all the interpretative angles of a poem or a book of poems, the more we can do to make structurally evident our own underlying categories and assumptions, the more honest we are being about the baggage we carry into the work—and therefore, the more space we are leaving the reader to create their own interpretations, truly and authentically. This is not to say that clumsy, obvious, heavy-handed OSPs are not possible—of course they are, just as there are heavy-handed formal poems and heavy-handed free verse poems—but it is not the OSP structure itself that creates the limitation in such cases.

A final reason poets may not use OSPs is because we may sense that the leap to hypotaxis could open up whole new cans of worms, prompting extensive revisions of poems that had seemed to be finished. This line of thinking is—fortunately or unfortunately as the case may be—100% true. *Coven*, for example, was almost completed when I finally accepted that the book I had thought was going to be a thematically organized collection of mostly metrical poems instead needed to be shaped like a spiral moving through five sections strictly adhering to five different metrical patterns. Whoops! Once I realized the shape the book would have, I spent another eight years recasting the poems' meters, replacing them with other poems in the appropriate meters, and reorganizing and rearranging the sections. It was an overwhelming amount of work, but the process of seeing the poems come into their own through their new metrical context was so exciting that I never regretted my commitment.

Of course, most organizing structural principles don't involve extensive metrical recasting. And if you are truly excited about yours, you likely won't mind the extra time. If there was really a process that would show you deep new ways to revise your poems and bring them to new levels of excellence, wouldn't you take it? After all, if you can't strive for perfection in poetry, where can you? I like to consider every setback or delay in publication, in the long run, as a gift, an irreplaceable opportunity to improve the book still further. *Coven* is only now becoming finished, after having been in process at least fifteen years. Why rush? As Yeats said, when we revise a poem, it is ourselves that we remake. I always advise poets to wait as long as they like before publishing a book. Once it's in print, it will be too late to improve it. And while I've heard many poets complain that they published a book too early or before it was really done, I have never once heard a poet complain that they waited too long to publish.

If you are interested in experimenting with an OSP for a poetry manuscript and aren't sure where to start, the three-step process used for Wilderness's book should be helpful, especially if you keep the following guidelines in mind:

For the first step, "notice patterns," you will only be gathering information. Your sole duties are accurate observation, full record-keeping, and an open mind. Have paper ready (I recommend three-dimensional paper for this, not a screen), and maybe a few different kinds and/or colors of writing implements. Read through your manuscript as if you've never seen it before, writing down anything that attracts your attention and repeats more than twice. Look for patterns of imagery (up/down, water, clothing, animals, locations, colors), types of language (words from different languages, turns of speech, levels of diction, noteworthy punctuation), unusual words that recur, poetic devices or forms, repeating themes or categories (historical periods, types of people, workplaces, imagery associated with areas of expertise or interest). If there are more than three examples, it's a good idea to jot them down as headings with lists of page numbers/line numbers underneath them. At this stage, resist the temptation to start dreaming about your OSP, because that might lead to ignoring something valuable. Just notice what patterns are there.

The second step, "use the patterns you've noticed to help you discover and choose a structure," is your time to dream. Take a new piece of paper and look over the patterns you've noticed, seeing what calls to you as a possible OSP. Maybe it will be the sounds of a group of words that you are suddenly excited to imagine as section headings. Maybe it will be a special group of images that you feel called to honor, to elevate, by allowing poems to crystallize around them. When you finally hit on a pattern that feels authentic, you will recognize it through a sense of excitement and, above all, curiosity. Do you wonder how the Table of Contents will turn out if you organize the book that way? Are you eager to reshuffle the manuscript and discover how those poems would look grouped together? Do you feel jazzed about how this new structure might impact the revising of your poems? An organizing principle that is forced can feel as if it is shutting things down or oversimplifying; but one that is authentic will feel as if it is opening doors into greater mystery and depth.

When contemplating a possible OSP, consider its symbolic resonance, your familiarity with it and feelings about it, and how it connects with the themes and topics of your book. Study it until you understand it deeply. Look up its etymology or those of its associated words. You may also want to weigh its mathematical or geometric resonance. What is its overall shape? Is it circular, like a clock, or meandering, like a river? Does it contain smaller shapes, like a snowflake? Does it have a few large parts, like a decade, or many smaller parts, like a year? What are the meaningfulness and effects of the limitations it imposes? Are the distinctions between its different parts maybe a bit fuzzy around the edges, like the Seven Deadly

Sins, or quite distinct, like the Three Fates? All of these qualities may end up affecting not only your book as a whole but the individual poems.

For step three, "develop your chosen structure further, to make its pattern(s) more evident to yourself and the reader," it's time to dive in and see how your prospective OSP works in action. Here's the basic principle of structural repetition, something to keep in mind as you rearrange the manuscript: put things that are alike into analogous places to create repeating, predictable structures. Check out all the tools you have available in your manuscript—table of contents, dedication, section titles, poem titles, epigraphs, footnotes, appendices, and so on—and remember that just because a poem has been published in a journal in a previous form or under a previous title, that doesn't mean it has to stay that way.

Finally, give yourself free rein to play, and do your best to turn off your inner critic. Especially if you've spent time in an MFA or other academic creative writing program, the critical inner voice can be disarmingly strong where anything involving poetic repetition is concerned. This is why poets who work with me to learn meter and form often report inner voices insulting them with words like "silly," "stupid," "babyish," and "embarrassing"; after one such online workshop, I tweeted from @poetrywitch: "Revelation arrived at by my class of (women) poets after a workshop in #deepform: In patriarchal culture, the need for order is feminized and reviled as weakness, a threat to individual ego…" If you find similar internal voices attacking your rearrangement of the manuscript, talking to them can be helpful. My inner critics respond well when I thank them first. A little speech (saying it aloud won't hurt) like this usually works pretty well: "Hi, inner critic. Thanks for your input. I know you're trying to protect me, and I appreciate it. I hear you, and I'm ok; I've got this. It's time to stop now. You're dismissed. Don't say anything else." If all else fails and your efforts at creating predictable symmetries in your manuscript still meet resistance, try repeating this motto, the teaching I most hope to convey to the poets I work with: "it's ok for my poetry to feel good in my body."

Now that I acknowledge how an organizing structural principle can change not only one of my books but also the individual poems in it radically for the better, I always aim to keep a manuscript of poems-in-progress. Even if the poems are so few and raw that the book may not be done for a decade, I start assembling it anyway, for three reasons: (1) revising a poem in the context of my other poems, similar to the way it will ultimately appear in a book, gives a complex creative jolt to the revision process; (2) it may take quite a while to hit on the book's best organizing principle, so the sooner I start exploring potential structures the better; (3) revising poems as part of a manuscript works nicely; I know where they are, and revising one poem leads smoothly into revising another. Two other poets I know seem to agree: Maxine Kumin once told me she kept her poems-in-progress in a single document on her computer desktop and scrolled down through the document to revise them, and Tim Seibles showed me a loose-leaf notebook full of printed poems-in-progress that he carried with him.

My book revision process tends to happen in waves; I will work through a printed copy of the manuscript with pencil or pen in hand (lately I prefer high-quality artist's pencils; they are cheaper, neater, work well upside down, and they are far better for the environment). I make tons of changes on some poems—deleting big chunks, reordering stanzas, changing the meter, and so on—and none on others. Once the process is done, I'll enter all the changes into the manuscript and print it out once again, typically removing the previous version from my favorite clip binder to make room for it (the previous version gets paper-clipped together and dated to be saved; my archive in the Beinecke Library includes dozens of manuscript versions for each book of poetry with many different contents and titles).

Of course, certain poems need a lot more attention than others. When it becomes clear that a poem is ready for an intense overhaul, I will copy the current version from the book into a poems-in-progress file in my favorite writing program (Scrivener), where I can make multiple revisions and easily save the major drafts in an organized fashion and print them out. I print drafts, edit them, and reprint them for as long as it takes—days, weeks, months. When the poem seems finished for the moment, I'll copy this "final" version back into the manuscript. This can be an exciting moment and sometimes leads me to print out the manuscript again, just to see how the new version of that poem looks in the freshly edited context of the book.

While sometimes I'm in such hot pursuit of a new vision of the manuscript that I open a newly printed version right away, just as often a major revision session—by "major" I mean one that culminates in printing out the book again—creates a gift for my future self. My writing life is full of many book projects, and putting a manuscript aside brings the mysterious force of momentum into play, adding an element of torque to the dance among revision, publication, and promotion. I love the feeling of having a completed manuscript of poems ready to look at, like a present waiting to be unwrapped. I love the feeling that every day the book is getting better and better, without me having to do anything but wait until the right moment, when I will have forgotten it enough to revise it freshly with the perfect mixture of curiosity, openness, and ruthlessness. That moment might happen three or four or six months later, when the journey of life has given me new insights or perspectives, or newly completed poems, to add to it; or when fate affords me a long plane ride or other perfect quiet window of time for a secret liaison with my most intimate lover—the current book.

Since I discovered the use of structural organizational principles, my relationship with my poetry manuscripts has become deeper and more complex, and it's no exaggeration to say that some of the most ecstatic moments of my life have happened during these moments of creative connection with my books of poetry. It's pure gold revision time, and so hard earned (through all the previous work on the poems) that I would never waste a second. I've learned the hard way to warn anyone who's in the house with me: "I'm going to read through the manuscript now. Please don't say anything to me until I tell you I'm done." And still, I seek out a safe place, just in case, because I know how intensely damaging an interruption can be. It's not just that I'd have to go back and start over from the title page, even if I'm already halfway through the book; it's that it might take hours if not days to regain my inner equilibrium and creative trust.

So I find privacy, and I sit down with the manuscript. Just holding it starts me down the path into strong trance. It's a fragile yet powerful condition, like holding a sacred flame. It's similar to the feeling I have reading a favorite poem by a poet I love, but exponentially more potent. The mood starts to constellate as I hold the manuscript and strengthens as I read, with intention, the outer title page. Like a thread growing stronger and thicker, it builds through the inner title page, the dedication, and the table of contents (of which I read every word, in order). By the time I begin the first section, I have become one with this connecting thread. My heartbeat and breath have slowed, my senses are hyper-attentive; in body and heart and spirit and mind, I have become nothing but one ear—an inner ear that can hear only one internal sound: the sound of this exact book.

The book and I dance across lifetimes, meeting each other newly in different guises in each section. The sections keep me deeply engaged, always aware of where I am not only in a poem and in the book—in the leaf and in the tree—but also in the pattern of the cells of the leaf, the web of interconnecting sub-parts. The patterns and rhythms and tones of each word reverberate within me in currents that carry me onward into the end of the section and build the exact vibration through which the section will come to its close and render me ready to enter the following section. The experience is visual and tactile as well as audible. Everything is heightened. If something is off, unfinished, confusing, or simply not finished in some way, I may feel it or see it before I even hear it.

The same process of revision that happens within each poem is also happening at the level of the sections and of the book as a whole. The main reason I can't be interrupted is that I'm holding the whole book in my awareness at once and I'm stretched to the max, just at the edge of losing a part of it. In addition to revising individual poems and rearranging them within or between sections of the book, or developing new sections and patterns, I might combine two or three poems into one. Or an element from one poem, such as a pronoun or punctuation mark, might find its way into other poems in the same section, opening them up into new dimensions as the section further develops its own identity and vocabulary. All the while, as in a living tree, the different parts of the book's identity seem to hold space for each other, keep aware of each other.

Being in the presence of other poems within an overarching structure seems to give poems permission to evolve, to discover new aspects of themselves—whether in form, voice, tone, or meaning. And the same can be true for the OSP itself. As your manuscript changes, it might become clear to you that the current organizing structural principle is simply not working, for one reason or another, and needs to be discarded like ballast. For many of my own various poetry manuscripts the structuring principle has changed several times, and along with it the central principle of each section, the poems in each section, and the title of the book. This has not been a problem for me; when it happens, I'm always so excited about the new idea that I'm happy to move on.

To develop an organizing structural principle for your poetry manuscript may not always be easy. To keep the big picture and the details in mind simultaneously, while doing both justice, requires will power, clear awareness, creative stamina, emotional vulnerability, and willingness to give up a measure of ego-control in the service of something larger. But if you are the sort of poet this approach will benefit, you may already be recognizing that the effort can be well worth it. Like completing a poem by discovering its structure through pattern, completing a book through an organizing structural principle adds a depth of authentic power and genuine accessibility that extends far beyond each individual poem.

As you discover which aspects inspire you the most, you may find that clear organizing structural principles at the level of the book, just like meter and other organizing structures at the level of the poem, can offer a poet immense wellsprings of creative inspiration. And of course, even if you end up not wanting to structure your book with an organizing principle, the very process of looking for one is sure to help you understand your manuscript far better.

3 Practices from *A Poet's Craft* *

"Mini-Book." Take three of your poems and arrange them in various orders. How does the experience of reading them differ, depending on the order?

"T.O.C. Spy." Examine the tables of contents of nine books of poetry. What do you learn about the poet simply from this, without looking at the rest of the book?

"Stylistic Analysis of a Book of Poetry." Write an essay four to five pages long consisting of detailed observations (generalizations backed up with quotes) about the styles and techniques used in a book of contemporary poetry. What are the poet's usual themes? How does the poet write about them using line length, form (meter, fixed forms, accentual verse, free verse), stanza, refrain, repetition, expressive variation if the poet writes in meter, line breaks, enjambment, word-music, diction, type of rhyme if any, voice, point of view, imagery, allusions, echoes of other poets' styles? Which aspects of their style do you like and want to emulate?

*These practices are taken from the end of Chapter 21 of *A Poet's Craft: A Comprehensive Guide to Making and Sharing Your Poetry*.

Works Cited

Coleridge, Samuel Taylor. *The Collected Works of Samuel Taylor Coleridge: Biographia Litteraria*. University of Michigan Press, 1931.

Finch, Annie. *Calendars*. Tupelo Press, 2003.

———. *A Poet's Craft: A Comprehensive Guide to Making and Sharing Your Poetry*. Wesleyan University Press, 2013.

Joyce, James, *Collected Poems*, Read & Co, 2014.

———. *Ulysses*. Oxford University Press, 1998.

Sarchild, Wilderness. *Old Women Talking*. Passager Books, 2017.

Starhawk. "Permaculture and the Sacred: A Conversation with Starhawk." Harvard Divinity School, Harvard University, March 18, 2013.

Valery, Paul. "Poetry and Abstract Thought." *The American Poetry Review*, vol. 36, no. 2 (March/April 2007), pp. 61–66.

The Shapes of Books

Stephen Kampa

AS ONE WHO sometimes struggles to find the shape of his own books, I come to a conversation about arranging a manuscript with a modicum of combativeness. By my lights, a book is a delivery system for the real goods: good poems. After all, for most poets, poems are what survive; books, by contrast, fall away like the husks that held the grain. Still, I find the shapes of books fascinating, and my purpose here is to propose some ideas about those potential shapes and to examine a few books in light of them. I do this not to advocate for the superiority of one approach; rather, I want only to make room for options, and to do that, one must know what the options are.

First, I submit that books perform two essential functions: the collocative and the generative. These functions relate to priority. When poems come first, the function of the book is to collect those poems in one place, perhaps identifying some principles for arranging the book into sections. That is, the collocative function puts extant poems in meaningful relationships: one looks out the window; sees a bird; thinks, *Wait, that's not a bird*; writes, "Bird thou never wert," etc.; and places that poem with others similar in prosody, theme, style, or sensibility. By contrast, when the book comes first, the function of the book is to generate new poems, whether that be because the book is a so-called "Project Book"—one that narrows its focus or procedures in predetermined ways and thereby also predetermines the kinds of poems that will be included—or because a book-in-progress has suggested to the poet poems that might be written to complement what is taking shape. That is, the generative function identifies in advance a book-wide subject or approach ("All of these poems shall be about hands" or "All of these poems shall only use the vowel *e*") or a book-based need ("I need more poems on birds" or "Boy, I could use a short buffer poem between those two long poems"), and the poet's job is to fill the order.

Second, I believe books can lean more toward the collocative or the generative function, and I believe a reader can infer *which* function from the shape of the book itself. Obviously collocative books include anthologies, especially those without calls for submission (and thus no poems generated specifically for the anthology), and the *Selected Poems* of most poets. Such books by their nature do not precede the poems but rather put them into a meaningful relationship; for instance, in the latter case, the poet (or editor) means to suggest a chosen batch of poems exhibits the highest quality or suggests the furthest reaches of a poet's talent and thus best argues for the poet's relevance to the culture. Although a *Selected* may seem fundamentally different from an individual volume of poems, and thus not useful for arranging a manuscript, individual collocative-leaning volumes follow similar principles: as the dust jacket copy of Richard Wilbur's *Things of This World* (1956) puts it, "Richard Wilbur...has now made a selection from his work of the past five years." (That he selected according to quality and range seems obvious: the book won both the Pulitzer and the National Book Award.) A single volume thus can function as a little anthology of the self, a *Selected* drawing not from previous books but from a body of hitherto uncollected poems. Particularly instructive here might be Albert Goldbarth's *The Kitchen Sink: New and Selected Poems, 1972–2007*, which organizes its selection partly by chronology (as do many *Selected* volumes) but also partly thematically: "[P]oems within the four chronologically determined sections...are *not* in original sequence of composition," Goldbarth writes in a prefatory note. "I've tried instead to reach a balance between the urge to consolidate like-minded themes and strategies, and the desire to be as various as that permits" (xix). Those qualities Goldbarth identifies—temporal continuities, "like-minded themes and strategies," and "the desire to be . . . various"—also apply to single volumes and can unite what might otherwise seem a disparate group of poems. Thus, when I read a book composed of multiple sections or suites that demonstrate both unity and variousness, I suspect I am reading a collocative-leaning volume.

I suggest that preeminent among these unifying qualities in a colloc-ative-leaning volume is time, which is why another indication of colloca-tive leanings is a subtitle including years: while Richard Kenney titled his first three collections *The Evolution of the Flightless Bird*, *Orrery*, and *The Invention of the Zero*—each of which demonstrated formal and thematic unity, so much so that the latter is arguably a single, book-length poem— his fourth and fifth collections were titled, respectively, *The One-Strand River: Poems, 1994–2007* and *Terminator: Poems 2008–2018*, suggesting that what unites the body of work is the poet composing over time. The books have a rich and interesting architecture, to be sure—I do not mean to imply the collocative function results in chaos—but that architecture seems decidedly more discovered than determined.

Finally, we might note how some writers have talked about their own book-shaping practices. Larkin famously remarked about the ordering of poems in his books, "I treat them like a music-hall bill: you know, contrast, difference in length, the comic, the Irish tenor, bring on the girls" (qtd. in Thwaite xi). That variety-show metaphor suggests a collocative function— one imagines a talent scout scouring local venues or an impresario audi-tioning local hopefuls, each trying to choreograph a lively spectacle of discrete performers with established routines.

I believe a reader can also infer a book's generative function from its shape. These books seem easier to identify. When someone encounters Christian Bök's *Eunoia*, I doubt the reader peruses page after page of poems using only one vowel and imagines that Christian Bök, looking in his heart as his Muse advised, sang songs of one vowel over and over and then thought, *Oh, wait, maybe I should put all these together.* We see such procedural books, or Project Books, all over the place. Amy Newman's *Fall*, according to the catalogue copy, "explores as its formal structure the seventy-two definitions for the word 'fall'" ("Fall"); and Richard Carr's

Mister Martini consists, according to the cover copy, of poems that "pair explorations of a father-son relationship with haiku-like martini recipes"; and Cole Swensen—well, Cole Swensen has made a career out of such books. The University of Iowa Press copy for *The Book of a Hundred Hands* says, "In this dazzling collection, Cole Swensen explores the hand from any angle approachable by language and art," and describes the work as "[i]ncorporating sign language, drawing manuals, paintings from the fourteenth to the twentieth century, shadow puppets, imagined histories, positions...and professions" ("The Book"). I note that in all three of these examples, some version of the word "explore" occurs, supporting my supposition that these books performed a generative—or, as we might also put it, exploratory—function.

In addition to the shapes and dust jacket promptings of such books, we might also consult the words of writers. H. L. Hix, in an interview with Karen Schubert, says,

> The first thing I'd say is that for me the basic unit of poetry is the book, rather than the individual lyric. That's how I most often read poetry (by buying books of poetry and reading them cover to cover), and I tend to respond especially strongly to "collections" that seem as though they were conceived as a whole rather than merely gathered and arranged as a concession to the obligatory publication format, whether old standbys such as Ted Hughes's *Crow*, longstanding favorites such as C. D. Wright's *Deepstep Come Shining*, or newer "discoveries" such as Patricia Smith's *Blood Dazzler*. Consequently, that's how I tend to write poems.

In this response, Hix identifies both the generative ("conceived as a whole") and the collocative ("gathered and arranged") functions, albeit with a clear preference. I also note the crucial element: Hix says, "[T]hat's how I tend to write poems." The book itself is generative.

Third, I suspect that all books perform both functions to differing degrees. Here, I offer my own experience. When I sent my third book to Waywiser Press, it was a gathering of poems I had written over the years that had not yet found homes in a book. When I had the post-acceptance, pre-revision conversation with my editor, Joseph Harrison, he suggested not only that I reconsider the arrangement of the book (collocative), but also some of its contents (generative). He and the other readers felt some of the best work consisted of short, sharply turned lyrics, and he suggested the book could use a few more. Although I am embarrassingly belligerent about line edits, I welcome book-level feedback, so I went to work: I removed a few long, shaggy poems and replaced them with shorter lyrics that I pulled out of old binders and polished up for the occasion. In what might be the strangest generative function of the book, I realized after I had written the jacket copy for it (ssshhh, don't tell), I liked its conceit enough to turn said jacket copy into the final poem of the book ("What the Rain Says"). Not just the book but the book production process—nay, the very *book jacket!*—generated a poem for the collection.

Fourth, I want to suggest that these two functions, the collocative and the generative, have an essential influence on a book's coherence. I recognize this as a tricky term. All books, provided they are not multi-author anthologies, exhibit the basic coherence of being products of a single sensibility, one that may use a surprising variety of aesthetic, rhetorical, figurative, philosophical, or prosodic approaches. Latent in the word *cohere*, however, and in some of the words the *OED* uses to define it—I'm thinking here of definition 4a, "To be *congruous* in substance, tenor, or general effect; to be *consistent*" (emphasis mine)—is the essential element: both the *co-* and *con-* prefixes suggest *togetherness*. What holds the book together? Are the poems gathered together for a cause like protestors, out of mutual affinity like a circle of friends, for focused conversation like a book club, due to a shared aesthetic like opera goers, due to demonstrated ability level like a sports team, due to contemporaneity like schoolchildren, due to a shared progenitor like a family, or simply because they exist in a broken world like members of a church, each of them welcome exactly as is and with no other requirement besides a common humanity—er, poeticality? I submit that many generative books answer the question of togetherness more clearly, and thus exhibit greater coherence, than collocative books. Whereas a primarily generative book wears its togetherness on its sleeve—for example, every poem in Greg Williamson's *A Most Marvelous Piece of Luck* is (a) a sonnet that (b) offers a mock definition of its title and in which (c) the "you" of the poem dies at the volta and (d) the last word is, again, the title—a primarily collocative book might place poems together simply because the same person wrote them, and perhaps around the same time.

(Hix suggests as much when he describes such books as "*merely* gathered and arranged as a concession to the obligatory publication format" (emphasis mine). Helpfully, his remark reminds us that books, in addition to being poetic gestalts, are also commercial objects limited and defined by their commercial contexts. This, too, shapes books in ways poets probably prefer not to admit.)

The point of thinking about books as leaning toward the collocative or the generative, and to consider what coherence this affords them, is (again) not to advocate for a particular model, but rather to articulate options, especially since there may come moments in a writer's life when a primarily collocative book asserts an identity beyond products-of-my-sensibility or these-are-all-my-poems-lately, inviting into its pages poems written specifically to tie together key threads in the book. As someone who has never written a primarily generative book, I can only speculate about whether the reverse is true, but I suspect it is: a poem long orphaned finds its home, at last, in a book that had up to that point been conceived and written as a Project Book. I keep as one of my personal pearls of wisdom tacked up on my corkboard this one from Fairfield Porter: "When an artist pays the closest possible attention to the work as it goes along, it does not escape his attention that the accident may have a place" (qtd. in Lehman 31).

In the brief discussions that follow, I want to look at books in light of these ideas with an eye to the perks and pitfalls afforded by their chosen shapes. From the outset, one thing I can say with certainty: the success of the book depends—always, always, always—on the excellence of the poetry.

• • •

To speak generally but, I hope, pertinently, I suggest a Project Book risks two main varieties of failure: a failure of conception and a failure of execution. Surely all books undertake these same risks, but the Project Book announces its ambitions and procedures more clearly than a catch-all collection of poems, thereby allowing readers to judge more accurately whether the book has succeeded on its own terms. A failure of conception might be as obvious as the book's animating premise—I see little hope for *A Poetic Taxonomy of North American Leech Species* (have at it, Mr. Goldbarth!)—or as subtle as structural deficiencies only noticed in consideration of the many ways the book *could* have been written ("Wait, wait, you could have organized the leech poems according to ascending bite radius!") By contrast, failures of execution are often immediately recognizable: lines fall flat, poems go nowhere, the poet exhausts the premise long before the book has been completed.

Rachel Hadas's *Poems for Camilla* is a Project Book, and both its animating premise and thematic thrust are clear. The book comes into being with the birth of Hadas's granddaughter, the eponymous heroine of the collection whose name derives "from *Aeneid* VII's warrior maiden, / the speedy runner, skimming over wheat, / scouring the ocean, keeping her feet dry" (1). This invites the poet to consider the many connections between our twenty-first-century world and Virgil's first-century one. All but one of the poems are preceded by an untranslated excerpt from the *Aeneid*, and most of the poems gesture back toward those Latin lines. This, then, is the book's conception. As a conception, it does not strike me as particularly novel, but it certainly has the sturdiness of received wisdom about it: *plus ça change, plus c'est la même chose* (which is as close as I get to Latin, alas).

However novel, sturdy, wise, or winsome the conception, a book must ultimately succeed by its execution, and it must do so poem by poem. Hadas's poems work in a variety of ways. Some draw striking or whimsical connections between the past and present, as when a Virgilian passage referring to the Sybil is followed by a poem about the poet's messy office being stirred by the winds of some new arrival: "Who's knocking? A delivery? A gift? / Another manuscript to blurb, another / request for a letter of recommendation?" (6) Others act as glosses or elaborations upon the Latin text, a sort of imaginative extension or analysis of the passage. "In Vain" reads like a brief versified piece of criticism comparing Virgil and Lucretius through their use of the word *nequiquam* and gently reproving another translator for having missed the subtleties and possibilities of Virgil's line (15–16). Most often, however, the Virgilian excerpt prompts rumination.

This rumination threatens to bury Hadas's finest effects and wittiest turns of phrase. "Tell me," she writes, "do the gods implant / this ardor in our minds—is it an add-on?" (14), and the pleasure of the musical response of "add-on" to "ardor" brings delight. She quips, with grammatical wit reminiscent of Heather McHugh, "The underworld is overrated" (33). She concludes another poem, "Worry matching worry, stride for stride, / you pace and talk together a long time," (8) and there is much to admire in these understated lines: the syllabic diminuendo of paired items ("Worry matching worry," with its three disyllabic words, connecting to "stride for stride" with its three monosyllabic words), the long polysyllabic word "together" in an otherwise monosyllabic line, and the slightly ill-fitting yet musically pleasing assonance of "stride" and "time." Out of such meticulous virtues, poetry is made.

Unfortunately, this poetry is often surrounded by a very different kind of writing, a rumination that seems to eddy and falter, unfinished. In these lines, Hadas considers some epic implications:

> Iapyx chose to learn the art of herbs,
> or maybe it chose him, for he was mortal.
> He didn't care about Apollo's gifts;
> he cared about his failing father. True,
> the herb that heals Aeneas' wound is plucked
> by Venus. Venus is Aeneas's mother.
> But Doctor Iapyx' story, as he struggles
> to find a perfect herb to fit the case—
> this is the poignant piece. (24)

Setting aside the inconsistency of using "Aeneas'" and "Aeneas's" in subsequent lines, I still can't help but hear these as versified lecture notes: one can imagine that were a professor to speak in stalwart blank verse to a classroom full of begrudging undergrads, it might sound something like this. Elsewhere, Hadas writes,

> Where do we go when we die?
> How much space will we take up
> and in which region of the afterlife?
> How will we be remembered, if we are? (30)

And elsewhere:

> Each person has their own particular day.
> We know what that means; know
> what will follow. Know and do not know.

> We remember and then we forget
> and need reminding and forget again.
> Each person has their own particular day,
> but shrouded in contingency. And fate? (29)

One might argue the repetition, unanswered questions, and fragments are a mimetic representation of thinking, but they also sound like a poet in the process of trying to find a poem. Such passages occur far too often in the book.

Perhaps not surprisingly, these large meditations on fate and the afterlife pale compared to the poems that consider daily life. "Looking On" compares Virgilian funeral games with present-day playground activities, collapsing a long lineage of watchful parents into four final words: "Riverside Park, Troy, Rome" (27). "The Long View" considers, well, the long view, but concludes,

> The angle of light shifts.
> Picnickers stand up and fold their blankets.
> Unfathomable mutability:
> Camilla will be three months old tomorrow. (28)

The invocation of the passing magic, or magic passing, of infant-calibrated time does far more work than "Unfathomable mutability," as a line, does. Perhaps the finest poem in the collection, however, remains the first, for it is there that Hadas captures both the animating impulses and emotions of the collection and, in a frightening way, those of our time:

> Curled-up morsel,
> you will uncurl those legs and start to stretch
> and then to crawl and then stand up and walk.
> And then, Camilla, you will start to run. (2)

• • •

Whereas Rachel Hadas relies on a generative premise that is essentially iterative—each poem takes up again the text of the Aeneid, enacting a meditative procedure that (ideally) results in some new insight about the relationship between text and world—Ilya Kaminsky relies on a generative premise that is accretive: *Deaf Republic* is a narrative, one in which a young deaf boy is murdered by soldiers in one of the first poems in the book. This renders the town deaf: as that early poem, "Gunshot," puts it, "The sound we do not hear lifts the gulls off the water" (11). (That sentence, by the way, embodies some of Kaminsky's clearest strengths as a writer: economy of language, metaphysical wit turned to serious purposes, wise silence, and a tone that is all hard angles and edges.) The rest of the book dramatically enacts the ramifications of this murder.

A few cautionary words are in order. Because many of the poems accrete power through narrative complication, some of them do not stand alone particularly well. A few, in fact, seem designed primarily to advance the narrative, which means that reading them is as satisfying as reading a brief chapter from the middle of a novel: if one is not aware of the preceding narrative and the implications for what might follow, one is likely to enjoy a finely turned sentence here or there while feeling that something is missing from what is ostensibly a self-contained artifact. This choice is perhaps doubly disorienting because the narrative is so episodic: it affects one as a series of minimalist pen-and-ink line drawings rather than as a fully developed oil on canvas. Additionally, while I would like to credit the narrative as a series of surprises, it is in some ways predictable: state-sponsored violence fells character after character, citizens resist (for instance, by strangling sex-distracted soldiers with puppet strings, which initially seems surprising, then doesn't), and eventually, the worst seems to have happened: "Our country has surrendered" (71). The most fascinating narrative element is the surrealist, figuratively resonant touch, the sudden town-wide deafness. Finally, the purposes to which the narrative is turned—to use that most horrifying of high school English words, its "themes"—seem not particularly surprising: we learn we are complicit in our silence; state violence makes puppets of us all ("Doors and puppets dangling from their handles, a puppet for every shot citizen" [68]), and despite all this, wonder may prevail:

> You will find me, God,
> like a dumb pigeon's beak, I am
> pecking
> every which way at astonishment. (30)

These few cautionary words seem appropriate given the extraordinary language used by the poet's champions, language which includes "world-changing publication" (Smith; and not even for this volume!), "I feel quite sure my grandchildren will read this book" (Porter) and "the most brilliant poet of his generation, one of the world's few geniuses" (Greenwell). Few things are more pernicious for an artist than overpraise. (A great poet, after being fabulously introduced at a reading I attended, began by saying, "Well, I'm going to try to live up to that.")

If neither the narrative itself nor the thematic implications of it are particularly surprising, what remains for the reader is what always remains for the reader, the poetry itself: the lines, the metaphors, the hard bright stones of memorable speech. Here I find the Kaminsky that those advocates, perhaps, see. His love poems can be understatedly carnal, as in these lines reminiscent of Yehuda Amichai:

Yes, I thieved her off to bed on the chair
of my hairy arms—
but parted lips

meant bite my parted lips.
Lying under the cool
sheets. Sonya!

The things we did. (23)

Yet Kaminsky also manages to praise quotidian miracles in the vulgar tongue:

Soaping together
is sacred to us.
Washing each other's shoulders.

You can fuck
anyone—but with whom can you sit
in water? (29)

For this reader, however, the Kaminsky that appeals most is the one of imagistic, metaphysical wit, the one who can write, "[I]n snow-drifted streets, I stand like a flagpole // without a flag" (70), the one who can write,

> On earth
> a man cannot flip a finger at the sky
>
> because man is already
> a finger flipped at the sky. (20)

There is hard-earned, luminous simplicity in such paradoxical figures, a simplicity that reminds one that *candor* is as much about white-hot heat as it is about truth-telling. Perhaps the most profound lines of the book— lines invoking theology, morality, complicity, and free will—are among its simplest: "At the trial of God, we will ask: why did you allow all this? / And the answer will be an echo: why did you allow all this?" (40). One notes that there need not be a god for the answer to come.

The poems that bookend *Deaf Republic*, "We Lived Happily during the War" and "In a Time of Peace," are among its finest standalone lyrics. The former acknowledges that "we // protested / but not enough" (3), that we lived in comfort while "around my bed America // was falling" (3), and it concludes,

> In the sixth month
> of a disastrous reign in the house of money
>
> in the street of money in the city of money in the country of money,
> our great country of money, we (forgive us)
>
> lived happily during the war. (3)

The accusation hits hard. Yet part of the book's brilliance, and one of the aims of its narrative, is to acknowledge how much the world invites us into love, courage, wonder, and even joy despite the rancorousness of history. The final poem, which juxtaposes a police shooting with the refrain "It is a peaceful country" (75–76) and a litany of daily errands, remembers this:

> I do not hear gunshots,
> but watch birds splash over the backyards of suburbs. How bright is the
>   sky
> as the avenue spins on its axis.
> How bright is the sky (forgive me) how bright. (76)

We have yet to escape the suffering we impose on each other by means of our so-called civilization, nor would Kaminsky have us remain silent before it; yet, as those words with their hard knowledge remind us, we cannot escape the brightness of the sky, either.

• • •

A third, even more tightly constructed version of the Project Book is one that aims to be a single poem, as is the case with Erica Dawson's *When Rap Spoke Straight to God: A Poem*. That subtitle is helpful: the table of contents contains four entries, suggesting individual units (sections or poems?), and within the book itself there are divisions, swerves, echoes, occurrences and reoccurrences of form, and stretches of blank page that might suggest separate lyrics, so the subtitle clarifies authorial intentions. The question a poem of this length—forty-six pages—invites is whether it hangs together rather than, say, disintegrating into a poetic sequence. Such a question seems particularly relevant for Dawson, whose first book, *Big-Eyed Afraid*, began with a suite of poems exploring her own notional nicknames, contained a variety of multipart poems (including a crown of sonnets, "Bees in the Attic," that only loosely separated each sonnet from the next, obscuring its sequential nature), and ended with a long, four-part poem or poetic sequence that used the warnings that come with pharmaceuticals as titles. All of this is merely to point out that from her first book on, Dawson has been interested in the ways poetic texts talk to themselves and to each other. Moreover, in addition to her impulse toward riffs, multipart poems, and sequences, Dawson also invokes the capital-letter Poetic Tradition regularly, meaning that for this polyvocal and deeply allusive poet, not all voices are her own. As she writes in *When Rap Spoke Straight to God*, "See, I have a thing for dead white guys. / Right now, Robert Herrick" (21). The collection has a natural, perhaps even necessary, culmination of these ambitious impulses.

Part of what holds the book together is not so much form as formal bravura, a virtuosic shifting between forms—some immediately perceptible, some not—in response to the shape of the moment's meditation. At least three sestinas unobtrusively—and it is a testament to Dawson's skill that one could use such an adverb for a sestina—weave thread-like through the text, as well as sonnets, rhymed pentameter quatrains, unrhymed tetrameter, and trimeter-tetrameter *abba* quatrains, the latter a form Dawson cultivated and used extensively in her first book and then revisited in her second. That revisiting, or perhaps repurposing, of stanzas calls to mind James Merrill's use of his own complex stanzaic invention from his first book's bird suite ("The Black Swan," "The Parrot," "The Pelican," and "The Peacock") in parts of *The Changing Light of Sandover*; in a more academic critical context, one might profitably write about Dawson's relationship to Merrill since her seamless shifting between forms is reminiscent of Merrill's technique and, further back, of Eliot's in *The Waste Land* and *Four Quartets*. (The enterprising essayist might even draw a connection through these writers to the Tennyson of *The Princess* and of *Maud; A Monodrama*, but such critical feats are beyond me.) What unifies the poem, then, is not a particular *form*, as in a sonnet sequence or *The Dream Songs*, but a formal *sensibility*, a sensibility both responsive to the immediate needs of the poem and cagily aware of the tradition in which the poem works.

That tradition is not only a formal one, but also a generic one: both Merrill and Eliot were in some ways doing the work of poetic cultural critics, and to that list I might add Melvin Tolson, whose rapid shifts in register, learned allusiveness, and musical savvy might have enriched Dawson's practice as well. For example, Tolson invokes, within fifteen lines, Blake, Shelley, Satchmo, and "a jam session / at the Daddy-O Club" (592–593); compare that with Dawson's invocation of Herrick, "Frost's birches" (12), "U-God from Wu-Tang" (1), Lil' Kim (38), and the register shifts of lines like these:

I be like, Damn, Virgo. Is this your jam?
Making your skirt look better than a bower,
your stomach's kind of parallelogram.

The sky is not a dome. There is no shelter.

I be like, Teach me what it's like to burn
in all the vapors, how to never swelter
so hot my core turns into iron's churn
and boil. Show me where you hide your blood. (10)

As implicit cultural criticism, these lines and poetic techniques (especially the all-inclusive allusive range) serve as praise for a kind of cultural and linguistic syncretism that is especially healthy: everyone—and every word—is welcome at the table. The point in drawing connections between Dawson and potential predecessors here is not somehow to diminish her accomplishment by suggesting the work or technique is derivative; rather, it is to place this book in its proper context, a context that includes some of the smartest poetry of the past century, in order to emphasize that this is a book that builds on the strengths of the tradition even as it acknowledges the failures of the past—for the past, and particularly America's sexist, racist past, have made for an almost unbearable present.

Here we have the second unifying element of the book: just as there is a formal sensibility managing the shift from sestina to sonnet, there is a humane sensibility trying to manage day-to-day consciousness in the all-too-dispiriting Trump era. (Indeed, one of the sestinas uses "trump" as an end word: "*Trump* / came out of *triumph*. Trump (verb): play a trump / on; win a trick" [13]) This humane sensibility weaves together memories—such as the speaker's initiation into sexual experience with a church camp counselor, "that one counselor awake, the one / with weed, listening to Snoop" (3)—and political concerns ("Bless this / matter. Black life, apparently, / now matters. Saw the effigy / on FB" [16]) and religious yearnings in an attempt to create some sort of sense, some coherent self in a world that seems bent on tearing so many selves apart. Whether such sense or coherence is achieved must remain debatable. Near the end of the poem, for example, two lines jumped out at me: "I can do all things / through ~~Christ which strengtheneth~~ me" (43). Perhaps that irreligious renunciation is necessary in our post-religious age, but I cannot see how it avoids the dangers of solipsism or of the will to power. Soon after that moment, Dawson gives us a vision, or an attempt at one, framed as a fragmented villanelle:

I see the exodus of light.
                    Let there
be black never absorbing white. Let there
be skin born black on every scar and tear. (43–44)

...

Let there
be not afraid, for you are with the fair
and mighty god of your body. (44)

Again, I worry about deifying the body (as opposed to embodying the deity): it seems to me an inadequate religious conception, one especially ill-equipped to deal with mortality. Yet I should acknowledge that this is not where the poem ends, although I will allow readers to encounter that ending on their own: it must be experienced as the fulfillment of the process of reading the entire poem, not as a quotation in a brief essay.

We cannot ask poets to provide a one-size-fits-all vision of the future or the good life. We cannot ask poets to chart the way out of the grotesque farce of a political landscape. What we ask of poets is that they testify—with exceptional eloquence, precision, and passion—to a singular vision of who we are and who we could be. This, Dawson does. Despite my reservations about overpraise, here I need to dispense with understatement: this is a complex, brilliant book, one that rewards rereading. Dawson has testified. We need to be listening.

● ● ●

At perhaps the other end of the spectrum from a book-length sequence based on the *Aeneid*, a book-length narrative about political complicity, or one long book-length poem, A. E. Stallings's fourth collection, *Like*, is a collection of discrete lyrics. Even the arrangement of the lyrics insists on their independence: as the dust jacket copy notes, "Stallings also eschews the poetry volume's conventional sections for the arbitrary order of the alphabet," putting her in the strangely overlapping company of both W. H. Auden and Dean Young, each of whom arranged volumes alphabetically. Of course, no order is arbitrary: alphabetical order invites a cluster of associations, including an index (a sort of authoritative source for locating), an "A-to-Z" reference work (another sort of authoritative source for explaining), and those aforementioned predecessors (is there a more authoritative source than W. H. Auden?). Perhaps most strongly, alphabetical order suggests that each poem is best considered not in conversation with adjacent poems but on its own terms and—this is where the ambition of such an arrangement shows—that each poem will survive such scrutiny.

Stallings is a technical virtuoso whether she cares to display it ostentatiously, as in the ending of "Alice, Bewildered," wherein Carroll's titular hero cannot remember her own name—"Liza, Lacie? Alias, alas, / A lass alike alone and at a loss" (6)—or to disguise it, as she does at the beginning of the prose-poem sequence "Battle of Plataea: Aftermath": "After the blood-brimmed field, we were amazed to stride into those empty silken tents—bright tapestries, wrought silver ornaments, the furnishings of solid gold. Eyes glazed at all the untold booty: gods be praised!" (11). Readers who read these sentences aloud might notice a certain sonnetty sound:

> After the blood-brimmed field, we were amazed
> to stride into those empty silken tents—
> bright tapestries, wrought silver ornaments,
> the furnishings of solid gold. Eyes glazed
> at all the untold booty: gods be praised!

(The nod to Frost's "A Silken Tent" seems a professional courtesy.) Stallings has other, far subtler methods of drawing attention away from her formal virtuosity. "Parmenion," one of several poems composed of five-line stanzas with varying line lengths, begins,

> The air-raid siren howls
> Over the quiet, the un-rioting city.
> It's just a drill.
> But the unearthly vowels
> Ululate the air, a thrill… (86)

The *howls/vowels* and *drill/thrill* rhymes are certainly audible, but the rhyme on *city* will not come to fruition until the penultimate monometer line, which reads in full, "A pity" (87). That distancing of rhymes is a common technique in Stallings, one that grants the musical and intellectual pleasures rhyme affords without as much risk of sing-songing. Indeed, whether or not Stallings is a poet's poet—her appeal may be too broad, and justifiably so, for that—she is a technician's technician, and any writer interested in new horizons for poetic form will need to consider her work.

Readers will recognize from previous books themes and rhetorical approaches that seem indicative of the writer's sensibility (which is one way we recognize our great writers: their work embodies a recognizable sensibility). Stallings is fond of collapsing the distinctions—or drawing the connections—between the daily or domestic and the mythic or meta-physical. In "Bedbugs in Marriage Bed," the metaphor announces itself early: "Maybe it's best to burn the whole thing down, / The framework with its secret joineries" (15). The clever indeterminacy of "the whole thing" and the polysemous precision of "joineries" are characteristic: hers are lines that immediately strike you with their rightness, then reward you with their richness. In this troubled marriage, there is no simple escape from the sense that something might be wrong:

> Who knows what eggs are laid deep in your dreams
> Hatching like doubts. They're gone, but not for good:
> They are the negatives you cannot prove. (15)

Although the poem opens up to a contemplation of the nature of doubt itself, is there a better encapsulation of such specifically *marital* second-guesswork? Stallings's metaphysical wit is as much on display in "Silence," which asserts, "Silence is a function of Time, the lark / In flight but not in song" (114). I have to curb my natural tendency to abuse exclamation marks when I read a metaphor as lovely as that. Although it is not a perfect book (and is there such a thing?)—"Cyprian Variations" seems uneven and long, and "Lost and Found" suffers from occasional fustiness—there are many, many pleasures to commend this excellent collection.

Great writers present a variety of selves. To return to Auden for a moment, there is the gnomic, public Auden of his early years and the gar-rulous, domestic one of the later years; although Jarrell famously preferred the former, I love the latter, and part of what makes the writer great is the capaciousness of the work, which accommodates these two separate loves from strangers. Moreover, this multiplicity of selves need not be a matter of chronology: as we conduct simultaneously our private lives, civic lives, religious lives, and so on, great writers explore all the facets of being that their gifts will admit to the page. It would be premature, self-serving, or both to declare A. E. Stallings a great writer here, but it is easy enough to see that she presents a variety of selves to her readers. The self that resonates most with me is not the Stallings of classical myth-(re)making, aesthetic meditation, or political protest; it is the one of intimate domestic chronicles, the one who puts words to our lived lives. This is not to say the other poems are no good; it is only to say that those domestic chronicles do a kind of work that is necessary, a preservation of the culture most likely to be lost to the future, the culture of a single family, in the idiolect of a single human consciousness wrestling with the immensity of the world and the paucity of our wisdom. Those poems do for me what the horses of "The Last Carousel" do for the poem's speaker, who is "moved by the pivot of their stillness, / By their ragged comet tails of genuine horsehair" (52). And sometimes multiple selves work by committee to create an exceptional poem, as they do in "For Atalanta," an apologia addressed to the poet's daughter. It begins,

Your name is long and difficult, I know.
So many people whom we didn't ask
Have told us so
And taken us to task.
You too perhaps will wonder as you grow … (47)

The explanation that follows interprets a myth for the daughter who, in the future, will be able to understand it, who perhaps will even live the life of "girls whose glories / Included rescuing themselves" (47)—for this is also a political poem, a poem acknowledging the dangerous political landscape of the present moment. Here we have the domestic chronicler, the classical mythmaker, and the political poet all in one. "For Atalanta" concludes in a way eerily evocative of Rachel Hadas's address to Camilla, for Stallings advises,

But it is not enough
To be nimble, brave, or fleet.
O apple of my eye, the world will drop
Many gilded baubles at your feet
To break your stride: don't look down, don't stoop

To scoop them up, don't stop. (48)

• • •

What can one say about the collocative and generative functions of books after looking at these four? While books that lean toward the generative (e.g., Project Books, though not only) exhibit much coherence and presumably can propel the poet beyond the blank page—as long as there are connections between the *Aeneid* and the experiences, observations, or ideas of the writer, for instance, or as long as there is more of Sonya and Alfonso's or Momma Galya's story to be told, there will be more poems— that is no guarantee the poems will be excellent or, in the case of narrative collections, even self-sufficient. Both collocative- and generative-leaning books rely heavily on a unified sensibility to lend them coherence: this is clear in Hadas and Kaminsky, which tend toward the generative, but even more so in the Dawson and Stallings. Although I have identified Dawson's as a Project Book, it also seems *less* like a generative-leaning one; that is, although the author has *asserted* the coherence of the book by making it one long poem, and although I can see myriad formal and thematic threads woven together, I also cannot pinpoint a generative principle. What seems to generate the poetry here is the crisis of a single self-and-sensibility faced with an unbearable cultural-political context, yet no particular procedure or form (that I can detect, anyway) determines the length or shape of the long poem. Instead, the poet has decided, ex cathedra, to present what might be considered, in other circumstances, a group of discrete, collocated lyrics as a single entity—much as the self, composed of various memories and mood, hangs together despite its variousness. That insistence on poetic unity in a poem about cultural divisiveness resonates powerfully. Finally, I note that even my assertion that a collocative-leaning book places poems in *meaningful* relationships was challenged by Stallings's arrangement, which insists instead on the arbitrary as a way to foreground not the book but the poem. All of this classification complication is good, as it reminds me that any classification falls short before the abundance and variety of that which it classifies.

It is a risky thing to infer how other poets write their books. Surely I have erred somewhere in my case studies and conclusions—at least, when it comes to the specifics of these books. Yet what I teach my students all the time is that we attempt to reverse engineer poems not because we want to find out how their authors wrote them, but because we want to figure out how *we* might have written them. Every new imagined process by which one might arrive at work is another potential avenue to success—not guaranteed success, but possible success. I think the same might be said of the larger unit of the book. If by looking at these books, and imagining what processes, procedures, predecessors, and provocations might have generated them, we arrive at a new method for ourselves, then the time is well spent, although I might add this: however many models you have at hand, and however much friendly help or editorial advice you get, only you can write your book.

Works Cited

Bök, Christian. *Eunoia: The Upgraded Edition.* Coach House Books, 2005.

Carr, Richard. *Mister Martini.* University of North Texas Press, 2008.

Dawson, Erica. *Big-Eyed Afraid.* Waywiser Press, 2007.

———. *When Rap Spoke Straight to God: A Poem.* Tin House Books, 2018.

———. "Fall." *Wesleyan University Press.* www.weslpress.org/9780819567093/fall/.

Goldbarth, Albert. *The Kitchen Sink: New and Selected Poems, 1972–2007.* Graywolf Press, 2007.

Greenwell, Garth. Cover endorsement for *Deaf Republic*, by Ilya Kaminsky, Graywolf Press, 2019.

Hadas, Rachel. *Poems for Camilla.* Measure Press, 2018.

Hix, H. L. "'Checking One Belief Against Another': A Conversation with H. L. Hix." *Agni Online*, 30 Jan. 2018, www.agnionline.bu.edu/interview/checking-one-belief-against-another-a-conversation-with-h-l-hix.

Kaminsky, Ilya. *Deaf Republic.* Graywolf Press, 2019.

Kampa, Stephen. *Articulate as Rain.* Waywiser Press, 2018.

Kenney, Richard. *The Evolution of the Flightless Bird.* Yale University Press, 1984.

———. *The Invention of the Zero.* Knopf, 1993.

———. *The One-Strand River: Poems, 1994–2007.* Knopf, 2008.

———. *Orrery.* Knopf, 1985.

———. *Terminator: Poems, 2008–2018.* Knopf, 2019.

Lehman, David. *The Last Avant-Garde: The Making of the New York School of Poets.* Anchor Books, 1999.

Merrill, James. *Collected Poems.* Knopf, 2001.

———. *The Changing Light at Sandover.* Knopf, 2006.

Porter, Max. Advance praise for *Deaf Republic*, by Ilya Kaminsky, Graywolf Press, 2019.

Smith, Tracy K. Cover endorsement for *Deaf Republic*, by Ilya Kaminsky, Graywolf Press, 2019.

Stallings, A. E. *Like.* Farrar, Straus and Giroux, 2018.

Swensen, Cole. Press copy for *The Book of a Hundred Hands*. University of Iowa Press. www.uipress.uiowa.edu/books/9780877459460/the-book-of-a-hundred-hands.

Thwaite, Anthony. Introduction. *Collected Poems*, by Philip Larkin, 1988, 1st American ed., Farrar, Straus and Giroux, 2004, pp. xi–xii.

Tolson, Melvin. "Lambda." *The Norton Anthology of Modern and Contemporary Poetry,* edited by Jahan Ramazani et al., vol. 1, 3rd Edition, W. W. Norton & Company, 2003, pp. 592–94.

Wilbur, Richard. *Things of This World*. Harcourt, Brace, 1956.

Williamson, Greg. *A Most Marvelous Piece of Luck*. Waywiser Press, 2008.

Writing on the Wall

A Mystery

Alyse Knorr

ORDERING A POETRY manuscript is a mysterious process. The best advice I've heard, from a poet to whom I am now married, is to arrange the order so that the poems can be at their most "devastating."

I married her because she says things like that.

But poets are usually not inclined to offer any advice on this subject. Given the dearth of craft writing on ordering a poetry manuscript, you might start to think that poets are superstitious about discussing it. Like if they try to pin down the mystery, it will slip away from them entirely. Maybe we feel exposed by the question—stripped of the words for an answer, naked. Ask a dog to walk on his hind legs, sure, but don't ask him to explain how he does it.

• • •

A professor of mine once suggested, only half-joking, that I throw my manuscript down a flight of stairs and use whatever order the pages landed in. I am not entirely opposed to this methodology.

• • •

Although it might not always seem obvious, I think most poets do know what we're doing, but not always how or why we're doing it that way. Maybe if you read enough books of poetry, you internalize the "feel" of a good order—a feeling described best not with logic but rather metaphor. The poet's native tongue.

So here goes: I've always preferred baking over cooking because baking has very clear steps to follow, whereas cooking requires more creativity and flexibility. I don't like going by "feel" because I usually don't trust my gut—on cooking and on many other things.

Manuscript ordering is more like cooking than baking. It is an intuitive process, not a logical one. When I'm ordering a manuscript, I get a sense that it feels good to move from one poem to the next, or that another pairing doesn't feel as good. If you asked me to pinpoint why some movements feel satisfying and others hollow, I suppose I could invent an answer. But the truth is that for me, ordering happens in this space of instinct and experiment. There is no recipe.

I have taken classes in piano, singing, acting, drawing, and tae kwon do, and at no point has my instructor ever told me to just "feel my way through" something or go with my instinct. But everything a poet does is rooted so deeply in self-trust that maybe this is the only advice worth offering about ordering a manuscript.

• • •

The version of Sylvia Plath's *Ariel* published in 1965, after Plath's death, is famously different from the version she intended. Plath's estranged husband, the poet Ted Hughes, edited the 1965 *Ariel*, and made many choices that deviated from Plath's original wishes. He added poems Plath wrote in the last few days of her life and had not intended to include, and he removed poems that personally implicated him—poems that mentioned his affairs or his leaving Plath and their children just months before Plath's suicide.

He also reordered the manuscript.

"To compare what we may call Plath's *Ariel* to the book that actually appeared—which is to say, to Hughes's construction of *Ariel*—turns out to be something of a shock," Marjorie Perloff writes (10). In Hughes's version of the book, the poems descend into chaos, sorrow, and despair, spinning out of control and suggesting that Plath's suicide was unavoidable.

But Plath's version of *Ariel* ends not in despair but in stoic optimism. The ordering scheme of Plath's version, Perloff writes, "moves *through*" (11, emphasis mine) Plath's heartbreak and anger at Hughes's affairs and then ends in "a ritual death and a move toward rebirth" (Perloff 11), in the form of a sequence of poems about bees.

The final lines of Plath's *Ariel* are:

Will the hive survive, will the gladiolas
Succeed in banking their fires
To enter another year?
What will they taste of, the Christmas roses?
The bees are flying. They taste the spring. (Plath as qtd by Perloff 16)

The final lines of Hughes's *Ariel* are: "We have come so far, it is over" (Plath as qtd by Perloff 16).

How many different potential books are contained within the same stack of poems?

• • •

Mathematically speaking, a collection of sixty poems has sixty! (that's sixty factorial) potential orders. That's a number with fourteen zeros at the end of it.

• • •

I know a poet who moves her furniture around often enough that every time I visit her home, it's brand new. Rearranged in new locations, the same pieces of art, the same chairs, the same books transform the whole.

• • •

At the end of the semester, my Advanced Poetry students each create a chapbook of their poems. They order the pages with a certainty and confidence that I can't help but admire. Their favorite part is sewing the books together, or stapling them with the extra-long stapler that can reach across the page spreads to the spines. They love the extra-long stapler. I watch them assembling their books in my classroom and think of Dickinson at her tiny desk in Amherst, carefully slicing up envelopes and sewing fascicles. Making, with her bare hands, a poetic artifact.

A book feels momentous. Fashioning a book where once there was just a pile of poems provides the same thrill as making a poem where there was once just a blank page. And so perhaps—if we must break with superstition and propose a theory—a poet should treat the ordering process like she would the composition of an individual poem. Treat the book like one long poem.

What would that mean, that philosophy?

• • •

I'm not the first to offer the suggestion. Robert Frost once said something like: if your book is twenty-four poems long, then the book itself is the twenty-fifth poem.

If we follow Frost's advice and think of the book as one long poem, then we can treat the movement from one poem to the next like a line break. Line breaks can create a feeling of friction or fluidity depending on what the poet wants them to do. The same is true of the movement from one poem to the next, which can create tension, surprise, juxtaposition, or an organic feeling of flow in an ongoing conversation.

In the same way that individual poems often benefit from having their first or last few lines lopped off, a poetry manuscript might benefit from cutting an overly explanatory "summary" poem from the end or removing an initial "throat-clearing" poem from the beginning and jumping right into the action.

When the poet to whom I am married read the first draft of my book *Mega-City Redux*, she recommended I cut the first thirty pages out entirely. "It's like you're warming up, or setting the stage or something," she told me. "Get to the point."

• • •

Allow me to get to the point. Like a poem itself, a poetry book finds its energy in the inherent tension between like and unlike: pattern vs. turns, repetition vs. variation, order vs. chaos. When the right balance is achieved, the poem—or book—contains a feeling of both inevitability and surprise. The surprise comes from the variations, or "unlikeness," and the sense of inevitability comes from the repetition, or "likeness."

Analogic or metaphorical "likeness" in a broader sense is at the very heart of how poems work—as Ariana Reines writes in *A Sand Book*: "Analogy is the structuring principle of the universe" (508). The likeness I refer to is echoic likeness—some kind of similarity between two poems in one manuscript that a reader will notice. For instance, two poems might use the same form—couplets, for instance—or employ a very similar tone. Or they might explore similar topics or use similar imagery.

Ordering a manuscript requires carefully considering when to put "like" together—creating pattern and harmony—and when to clash "unlike" against one another, creating juxtaposition and contrast. For instance, if one poem ends with an image of water, following it with a poem that begins with an image of water will create a natural, organic transition. Following it with a poem that begins with an image of fire will create an exciting juxtaposition or tension. Either can work—provided there's a broader sense of balance throughout the manuscript.

If all the poems in the book feel too randomly ordered—from too much unlikeness following unlikeness—then the book will lack cohesion. But if the order is hyper-controlled and overly planned, the book will feel too tedious to be devastating. In other words, clustering all of the book's water poems back-to-back in one section might get boring. Better to space them throughout, where they will feel both surprising and inevitable each time the reader stumbles upon one.

• • •

This is what Ross Gay does in his book *Catalog of Unabashed Gratitude*. Throughout the book, Gay sprinkles in poems explicitly identified by their titles as odes—some named "Ode to [X]" and others simply "To [X]." The first few entries in Gay's table of contents look like this:

To the Fig Tree on 9th and Christian
Ode to Buttoning and Unbuttoning My Shirt
Ode to the Flute
Burial
Patience
Ode to the Puritan in Me
Feet
Smear the Queer
To My Best Friend's Big Sister

After using three odes in a row to introduce the reader to the concept of the ode—and to his approach to it—Gay mixes in two non-odes, then a fourth ode ("Ode to the Puritan in Me"), then two non-odes, then another ode using the "To" titling scheme he started the book with. The rest of the book continues in this fashion, with "To X" and "Ode to X" odes scattered in amongst non-odes. Dispersing odes amongst non-odes preserves a sense of surprise in the reader every time they encounter one, and allows the odes to converse with other poems that use different conventions and tones.

Gay places a poem called "To the Mulberry Tree" toward the end of the book, providing a nice sense of unity with "To the Fig Tree on 9th and Christian" from the book's beginning. Gay's penultimate poem is the book's titular piece: "Catalog of Unabashed Gratitude," and his final poem is titled "Last Will and Testament." Gay creates a strong feeling of closure by ending the book with the highly anticipated title poem, followed by a poem whose name gestures explicitly toward finality.

• • •

I have tried to find the origin of the Frost quote, but it's missing. When I field the question on Facebook, I'm told its origins are untraceable and the story probably invented. One poet says: "This [quote] framed the theme of an entire AWP panel, but I think even they admitted it might be apocryphal, or paraphrased from a lecture."

• • •

If you're going to treat your book like one long poem, you'll need to be able to see it that way, in its wholeness. I mean literally see it that way—it's very hard to order a collection looking only at your computer screen. Instead, print the manuscript with no numbers on the pages, two pages to a sheet, and then cut the sheets in half so you'll have enough room to look at all of them at once on your table or floor or wall. An added benefit is that each page will be around the same size as pages in a printed book, reminding you that that is what you're doing here—making a book.

The best time to order your manuscript is after you've taken a long break from the poems—a few months is perfect. You'll have the emotional distance you need to make cuts, and you'll approach the poems a little more like a reader than like their author. The longer the break, the better.

Shuffle the pages around and then read all of them carefully out loud. You need to have a solid sense of what each poem is doing as an individual in order to think about their role in the book.

Lay the pages out on the floor, or pin them to a wall. Then, using colored pencils, markers, or highlighters, begin marking all the different repeating elements of the manuscript: any reoccurring key words, motifs, images, or themes. Track anything concrete that you do multiple times, using some kind of color-coding scheme.

Mark also any moments when an important piece of information is deployed. For instance, if you reveal in one poem that your mother is dying, and many of your other poems explore this grief, then pay attention to which poem reveals the information about *who* is sick and dying.

When you look at all the poems at once, you might notice a lot of one color clustered together. Try to spread that color out a little, so that all your "likeness" isn't piled on itself.

Move your poems around and read through them again and again. Each time you reach a place that doesn't feel right, swap that poem out for a new one and see if it works better or worse than the previous choice. All you need to know is if this choice is better or worse than before—it's like visiting the optometrist and comparing two lenses at a time until you arrive at the perfect prescription.

This stage is the mysterious part—the part that might feel more driven by the gut than the brain. Trust yourself. Or go find a staircase.

• • •

I lay out the pages of my chapbook manuscript in the hallway on the long blue runner rug. Strapped into a bouncer by the front door is my five-month-old daughter: supervising, bouncing, hurling her toys at my poems. I consult her for advice, showing her two different page options at a time, and mix into the order the ones she reaches for, laughing.

• • •

In the Vermont house where Robert Frost wrote some of his most famous poems, the walls are covered in writing. As part of a renovation to open the house up as a museum, painters etched some of Frost's poems and even his epitaph—"I had a lover's quarrel with the world"—onto the walls (Rathke). The four-stanza poem "Stopping by Woods on a Snowy Evening" is four feet tall. Black ink on a white wall (Rathke).

• • •

Another way to demystify the manuscript ordering process is by focusing first on the book's beginning and ending. Start by finding the poem you want to open the manuscript. This should be one of your strongest poems in the stack, and one that offers a sense of the main themes, questions, or topics the book will explore. Consider how the first word in an epic sets up the whole theme of the epic. The *Iliad*, for instance, opens with the word "rage," since that's what it's all about. The *Aeneid* opens with "arms and a man," because these are its main topics. Remember that readers will imprint like a baby bird on the first poem of the manuscript; they will assume that in some way, the whole manuscript will revolve around the themes, topics, and questions raised in the first poem. The first few poems—and the first poem especially—teach the reader how to read your book. Pay attention to how the poems at the beginning of the manuscript set up the themes, motifs, and characters that the book will explore. It doesn't need to establish all of them, though—you can save some to deploy later as complications or turns.

Pay close attention to the next nine pages, too. The first ten pages of your book must be excellent and keep the reader reading—especially if you're trying to publish the manuscript through a contest or open reading period—so put your best poems in front.

Once you've got the beginning figured out, find the poem you want to be close your book with: a strong poem whose final image, line, and word you think is particularly poignant and closural. Remember that closure isn't the same thing as "resolution." Syntactic, imagistic, and sonic closure—a "feeling" that the book has arrived at a satisfactory stopping place—is more important than a sense that all the book's questions have been answered. You may even have arrived at new questions by the end.

Now, as you order the middle of the manuscript, think about how your choices create a sense of growth or change. How does the order of the poems allow the reader to keep probing deeper and deeper into an idea or a question or a wound? What information is deployed in each poem, and what is the significance of the order in which the reader receives that information? What new questions, conflicts, or themes (which I often call "variables") emerge in each new poem, and what is the significance of that order? How does each poem build on, subvert, or complicate the previous poem? How does each poem set up the next? How is the end of one poem in conversation with the beginning of the next poem?

Remember that too much "like" side by side will get boring, so don't arrange poems by topic or form. In other words, don't stick all the love poems in one section and all the nature poems in another, or sequester free verse poems off from sonnets. Instead, let your topics and forms and approaches collide against each other and play together. Spread out poems with similar forms, themes, and topic, but don't feel like you can never have two similar poems, or poems with similar images, side by side. You can! It's all about the balance.

• • •

Gary Jackson's *Missing You, Metropolis*, published in 2010, pays careful attention to its beginning and ending. The book interweaves narrative poems about growing up and reading comic books with poems set in the worlds of those comics: poems from the point of view of Nightcrawler or Iron Man or Lois Lane.

The first poem in Jackson's book, "The Secret Art of Reading a Comic," begins:

The old comics were never wrong.
Right always defended
by the hero—polished like Adonis. (5)

With this opening, Jackson establishes some of the central themes of the book: justice, morality, rectitude, and heroism. The rest of this first poem catalogues a long list of superheroes and describes the panels, gutters, and word bubbles of comic book art, thoroughly introducing the reader to the book's central motif. The poem ends with the image of Captain America's sidekick Bucky falling to his death, revealing the perspective that Jackson will bring to comic superheroes in this book: one focused on the undercurrents of grief and loss in these seemingly simple heroic narratives and in the speaker's own life (6).

The second poem in the book, "Stuart," introduces the collection's themes of race and friendship, and introduces the reader to Stuart, a character whose loss—revealed at the end of the first section—will permeate the rest of the book (7). Jackson creates tension and foreshadowing by moving from the final image of the previous poem—Captain America's best friend dying during battle—to the introduction of the speaker's best friend at the beginning of the next poem. The third poem in *Missing You, Metropolis* introduces the fact that the speaker's younger sister died in childhood (8). By establishing Stuart and the sister early, Jackson can return again and again to these characters throughout the book, adding new complications and nuances each time he reveals them.

The final poem in *Missing You, Metropolis* is called "Reading Comic Books in the Rain" (81). Like the first poem in the book, this poem revolves around the image of the speaker reading a comic book, and returns to some of the first poem's imagery: panels, gutters, white bubbles. This return to where we started creates a satisfying sense of artistic unity. Only this time, the poem reflects on the rest of the book with a more meta perspective fitting for a finale: "Looking back, I realize // we should've stayed in that four-color world / a little longer. Escape for as long // as we could" (81). The poem's final lines serve as a kind of summary of the book's project and an overarching reflection on the greater significance of comic books, and, implicitly, poetry: "we indulge in the power / to inhabit a world a page removed from our own" (81).

• • •

The poet to whom I am married is flipping through my manuscript on the couch, reordering the poems with a speed and confidence that amazes me.

"How are you doing that?" I ask her. "What are your criteria for where to put them?"

"I don't know," she tells me. "You've been overthinking it."

• • •

Grant me intention, purpose, and design—
That's near enough for me to the Divine.

And yet for all this help of head and brain
How happily instinctive we remain.
—Robert Frost (425)

• • •

If your manuscript is narrative or loosely narrative, like Jackson's, then you must also consider when to introduce characters and when to intensify conflicts. Here again, using visual strategies to view the whole manuscript at once can help make the process feel less murky.

For instance, you can draw a reverse outline of your book, tracing the narrative or theme as it develops and writing out the timeline or character arc of what you've created.

In my first book, I mixed narrative poems set in a "real-life" present moment with first-person poems set in the protagonist's mind, ungrounded in any specific point of time (i.e. memories, dreams, or fantasies). Weaving these together required mapping a timeline of what literally happens in the narrative and what happens in the speaker's mind.

Mapping out the order like this allowed me to introduce foreshadowing, negotiate tense, keep track of what the "present moment" was, and pinpoint how the emotional, thematic, intellectual, and character arcs all aligned.

Ordering is messy. It's not like laying out an architectural blueprint for a house. When I reread my maps and ordering notes for my earlier manuscripts, they look like ancient runes that I can barely decipher. Scattered along the page are symbols and color codes that once meant something, when I was in the thick of each poem and all the poems.

• • •

I'm sitting by Edna St. Vincent Millay's emptied pool during a residency at the Millay Colony in upstate New York. The sun is bright and I'm imagining one of Millay's nude theater performances taking place on this very patio at one of her raucous summer parties. In my hand is a stack of poems I'm trying to order. My second book before it was a book: a collection of pages, unformed, ready to become something whole. I close my eyes, pray to Millay, and begin the sorting, feeling naked.

• • •

One advantage of the scattering technique is that every time the reader catches a motif sprinkled throughout the manuscript, they will experience the thrill of simultaneous surprise and recognition.

Now is about the time, for instance, that I should remind you of Robert Frost. Aren't you glad I've carefully dispersed him throughout? When he pops back again, doesn't it feel both surprising and inevitable?

• • •

In explaining how she assembled her intricate hybrid work *The Crying Book*, Heather Christle describes her initial sense of the book, before it took shape, in ghostlike terms: "a book was in there. But where were its edges?" The manuscript existed in an intangible space in Christle's mind, and she found herself unable to see it as a whole—only in glimpses. "Still," she writes, "I knew the whole was there, could sense the presence of its shape, even if it remained obscure to me."

Inspired in part by the way quilters plan out their designs on graph paper, Christle decided to map out her book on graph paper, coloring squares on the page so that each shade represented a certain thread, approach, or motif. The visualization allowed her to find balance. "I could see, at last, the whole, could see the gaps and oversaturation in the pattern," she writes.

For Christle, mapping out her book this way meant returning, procedurally, to a delightful physicality. "What a joy to move away from the screen and back to paper, the place where all my writing work begins," she says. "What absolute satisfaction to smell the pencils; to hear the soft sound of a square filling up with orange; to look, in the end, at something that didn't need time to be understood or experienced, that could be apprehended in an instant."

• • •

Why do my students love the long stapler so much? The long stapler marks the moment the poems transcend their individuality and start to become a book. When they move off a screen or out of a notebook and become an object, embodying the Greek word for poetry, *poesis*—a made thing. Like Christle says, this tactile, physical, embodied stage of the writing process is beyond just exciting—it's sublime, in an almost spiritual way. Painters and sculptors get to make objects—one-of-a-kind creations that can be bought and sold and never copied exactly. But words are infinitely re-transmittable, and therefore fragile and inconcrete. Once they've been gathered and formed into artifact, they then seem somehow finally real. No wonder poets are so superstitious about dissecting the process.

• • •

Won't this whole instinct matter bear revision?
Won't almost any theory bear revision?
—Robert Frost (279)

• • •

Don't stop after the very first order you come up with—try multiple versions of the order and see what works best. Maybe, in the end, that will be the first order, but it's worth seeing what the other options are.

When you've found an order you love, take the poems down from the wall or pick them up off of the floor. Stack them up in order and then sit down and read the book aloud to yourself from beginning to end. Make sure the order works well when you experience the book the way a reader will, one page at a time.

Once you've finalized an order, let it sit and return to it a month later to see if it still works. Time away from the manuscript is the most useful resource you can create for yourself.

• • •

Mónica Gomery's book *Here is the Night and the Night on the Road* is a beautiful collection of elegies whose ordering implicitly upends traditional cliché notions about the "stages" of grief. The book opens with the line: "To say I choose the world, and you in it" (1), an emphatically hopeful declaration of the speaker's autonomy in preserving the memory of the beloved "you." The beginning of the next poem admits the difficulty of the project ahead: "Because the story itself feels like too much to tell" (5). Right from the beginning, she has announced the book's key intentions and concerns.

From here, the book proceeds in three sections, with repeating titles like "Season of Elegy," "Confession," "Anger," and "Elegy" scattered amongst titles that occur only once. Gomery is not afraid to put two poems with the same title back-to-back, which reads to me like a gesture at how grief is not linear or regular in its trajectory. At times, it lingers. At times, it grows.

What I admire most about Gomery's ordering is the way she moves between sharply contrasting forms and tones. One page might be full of dense, justified prose while the page that follows it is airy and open, with only a few single lines jotted onto the space. She often juxtaposes a more experimental or lyrical approach alongside a direct, plainspoken tone with narrative elements and straightforward syntax. For instance, an experimental poem titled "Death Is" fills the page with ninety-nine instances of the words "extraordinary" and "ordinary" alternating back and forth (20). The next poem starts simply: "Here's how / I remember it:" (21) and begins narrating a remembered scene.

Gomery's ordering choices create a constant feeling of surprise for the reader via these shifts in tone and form, which balances well with her consistent focus on the central theme of loss. The rapid juxtaposition of different approaches to exploring grief seems to lend credence to the speaker's belief that "the story itself feels like too much to tell" (5), and adds a greater sense of urgency as the speaker tries technique after technique to cope with the loss. There's an aching sense that she's searching for different ways to articulate the emotions, and the order makes clear that the chaos of writing about grief follows no clear pattern through which to progress.

The order of the poems, in other words, is devastating.

• • •

Elizabeth Bishop said something similar to Frost, but grander. Bishop thought of *all* her poems as "one long poem" (Bishop as qtd by Treseler) In a 1947 letter to her therapist, Bishop wrote that after having envied the way that painters could "use the same material over & over & over again," she now conceived of her poems as overlapping and interconnected (Bishop as qtd by Treseler). Instead of thinking of each poem as a totally new, "isolated event," Bishop found that she no longer faced "the fear of repetition" (Bishop as qtd by Treseler). In a sense, then, Bishop's life—any life—is one long poem.

Seventy-one years later, Ada Limón said in an interview on manuscript ordering: "I have long wanted to structure a poetry book the way we might structure a life, the whole mess and breadth of a life. There are the small rise[s] and falls of the daily journey and then there are the larger plummets and big-ticket items that set us roiling like a sea" (Limón as qtd by Blake).

• • •

I'm ordering a manuscript during a residency at the New York Mills Arts Retreat in New York Mills, Minnesota, a town with a population of just over one thousand. It's so small and remote that I—a city person—have begun having nightly panic attacks. But here in the cultural center, the quiet is peaceful, purposeful. It's what I came here for: time and space. The knitting club is downstairs knitting, and I'm in the attic dance studio with an enormous papier-mâché sculpture of a blue woman watching me work. I lay out poems on the wooden floor. In the glass of the mirror wall, the poems and I are doubled. My manuscript blooms from 60 to 120 pages, and my authorhood splits in two.

This is what it means to turn a group of poems into a book—into one long poem. It means moving between consciousnesses: author and reader, logic and intuition, control, and trust. And it means embracing the mystery of the process. And so here in this room, in the middle of the long poem of my life, I am content to be wordless among my piles of words.

Works Cited

Blake, Sarah. "How Do Poets Order a Collection?" *Chicago Review of Books*, 1 Nov. 2018, https://chireviewofbooks.com/2018/11/01/how-do-poets-organize-a-collection/. Accessed 12 Nov. 2021.

Christle, Heather. "On the Patchwork Approach to Piecing Together a Book." *Lit Hub*, 5 Nov. 2019, https://lithub.com/on-the-patchwork-approach-to-piecing-together-a-book/. Accessed 12 Nov. 2021.

Frost, Robert. *The Poetry of Robert Frost: The Collected Poems, Complete and Unabridged*, edited by Edward Connery Lathem. Henry Holt and Company, Inc., 1979.

Gay, Ross. *Catalog of Unabashed Gratitude*. University of Pittsburgh Press, 2015.

Gomery, Mónica. *Here is the Night and the Night on the Road*. Cooper Dillon Books, 2018.

Jackson, Gary. *Missing You Metropolis*. Graywolf Press, 2010.

Perloff, Marjorie. "The Two Ariels: The (Re)making of the Sylvia Plath Canon." *The American Poetry Review*, vol. 13, no. 6, 1984, pp. 10–18.

Rathke, Lisa. "Visit the Vermont House Where Robert Frost Wrote His Most Poetic Lines." *WBUR News*, 21 May 2018, https://www.wbur.org/news/2018/05/21/robert-frost-museum-vermont. Accessed 12 Nov. 2021.

Reines, Ariana. *A Sand Book*. Kindle ed., Tin House, 2019.

Treseler, Heather. "One Long Poem." *Boston Review*, 17 Aug. 2016, https://www.bostonreview.net/articles/heather-treseler-elizabeth-bishop-foster-letters/. Accessed 12 Nov. 2021.

Some Assembly Required

Harvey Hix

Analogy

BOOKCASES LINE ALL four walls of the room in which I write this brief. They range in size (some stand waist high, some chest high, some head high); they arrived at my home in various ways (some I toted home in the trunk of my Toyota, some the UPS driver dollied to my door); their veneers vary (some mimic oak, some ash, some cherry). For all those ways in which they're mismatched, though, they do have this in common: I assembled them all. They're not the pricey solid-wood units I'd buy if I had more discretionary income, the kind that come from the furniture store already built, delivered in a box truck by husky college students working summer jobs. My bookcases weren't bookcases yet when I got them. They arrived in cardboard boxes, as bookcase parts: tightly packed lengths of pre-drilled particle board, cut to length, and heat-sealed plastic bags of screws.

Which means that in at least this one way each bookcase resembles any book of poems: it was parts, but got assembled into a whole.

Fortunately for never-been-accused-of-being-handy me, each box of bookcase parts included, on a single folded sheet or in a slender, stapled bifold booklet, easy-to-follow step-by-step assembly instructions. Unfortunately for always-at-work-on-a-poetry-book me, if anyone before now has written out equivalent instructions for assembling a poetry book, I've never seen them. It would be helpful to have such instructions, so as a first set, for others to modify and refine, I propose the instructions that follow. These poetry book assembly instructions do have points of analogy with the bookcase assembly instructions: they too are "easy-to-follow" and "step-by-step." They call for a disclaimer, though. For all their resemblance to the assembly instructions packed with the parts for each bookcase, these instructions differ from those in at least two ways.

First, the bookcase assembly instructions are intended to preclude judgment. They are meant to ensure that you don't have to "figure out" how to assemble the parts into a bookcase. The idea is that when you follow the instructions included in the kit you bought, and I follow the instructions in the same-model kit I bought, the resulting bookcases will be identical. When both of us go for a coffee to congratulate ourselves on work well done and return to find that someone has moved our newly assembled bookcases across the room from where we left them, it won't matter which bookcase you claim and which I claim: we won't be able to tell them apart.

These poetry book assembly instructions, by contrast, are intended to inform judgment. They are meant, not to relieve you from having to figure out how to assemble your poems into a book, but to enhance the order and focus of your thought processes as you do your figuring out. The idea is that following these instructions will produce a different result each time: when you apply these instructions to your poems and I apply them to mine, the resulting books will differ radically from one another. What we'll later go for coffee to celebrate is how different our books are from one another. We followed the same set of assembly instructions, but no one could mistake your book for mine, or mine for yours. Same assembly instructions for both, but each resulting book unique, inimitable.

A second contrast is that the bookcase assembly instructions are linear; these poetry book assembly instructions are circular. To follow the bookcase instructions, best to do step 1 first; don't skip to step 4, and plan to do step 1 later. (For at least some of the steps, you can't invert the order: you can't start by tacking the trifold imitation-woodgrain cardboard backing to the case, because there's nothing to tack it to, until you've first attached the sides of the case to the top and bottom shelves.) The order of steps is fixed, and the last step of the bookcase instructions completes the assembly: no point in repeating any steps.

To follow these book assembly instructions, by contrast, you might start anywhere: start at step 1 if you want, or at step 4 if you prefer. Select the poems first and then sequence them, or sequence them first and then select. Either way can work. Also, these book assembly instructions invite repetition, rather than precluding it. Repeat any given step, or the whole set as often as you like (or can manage): each repetition of any step in the assembly process should further refine the finished product.

Instructions

Subject to those disclaimers, here are some "Easy-to-Follow Step-by-Step Poetry Book Assembly Instructions":

1. Select the poems.

Assembling a poetry book always demands that the poet answer the question, Which poems will this book include, and which will it exclude? The principle(s) of inclusion/exclusion may vary widely from poet to poet and from book to book, though, so it helps, in working toward any given book, to be explicit about what the operative principle is in this particular case. If this book is my journal of the plague year, chronicling my life in COVID-19 lockdown, the principle will be to include poems written during that time, about that time, and to exclude poems written at other times, about other things. It doesn't matter that the poem I'm most proud of was published in *The Literary Review* and picked up a Pushcart, if that brilliant uncollected masterpiece was written in 2015, long before the pandemic, about the many friends I made aboard the crowded ship on my Caribbean cruise: I'll have to save it for my next collection, because it doesn't belong in my COVID book.

If the book I'm assembling is not topical in that way, the principle might be, say, simply to include the hundred poems I consider my best work, exclude the rest, and figure out later if the poems I've included all share a topic or theme. As noted above, both my choosing the principle and my applying the principle will involve judgment (does this poem belong in my best hundred? Is it better than this one?), but my decisions about what to include in and what to exclude from my book are likely to go better the clearer I am about what selection principle(s) I'm applying.

Application of a chosen principle of inclusion/exclusion might be constrained by parameters of inclusion/exclusion. If the contest to which I plan to send my book allows only entries that have between forty-eight and sixty-four manuscript pages, but I have two hundred pages of COVID poems, I'll have to supplement my selection principle, to get me from including two hundred pages to including no more than sixty-four, or I'll have to modify my hundred-best principle into my fifty-best principle. Even if the parameters are imposed on me in this way, so that only my selection principle is my own choice, being clear about both the principle and the parameters will help me make sound decisions about what to include in, and what to exclude from, my book.

2. Group the poems.

Another question that a poet always answers in assembling a book, and that it is well to answer deliberately and reflectively, is Will these poems be organized into a single, undifferentiated unit, or also clustered into sub-units? The analogous question for a novel would be about division into chapters; for a play, division into acts and scenes. Are there multiple "episodes" worth demarcating in my poetry book, or is it a single "event"?

Neither answer, one group or several groups, is inherently superior to the other: any of us could walk our fingers along our shelves of poetry books and pull out numerous favorites—books that matter to us—whose constituent poems are clustered into subgroups, and other favorites whose poems are not clustered. The question is which structure is most appropriate to these poems in this book. That observation highlights one feature of these instructions, one more difference from the bookcase instructions, to be added to the differences noted above: these instructions don't "pull apart" in the same way the bookcase instructions do. They can be distinguished from one another, but not separated from one another. When I am performing step 2 of the bookcase assembly instructions, attaching the left side panel to the base, I am only performing step 2. I'm not also performing step 1, attaching the right side panel: I've already done that.

Here, though, the step of selecting the poems for my book and the step of grouping them might depend on one another. My selection principle, a year of COVID poems, might not be independent of my grouping decision: it creates a possibility—subdividing the poems into twelve groups, one for each month—that wouldn't be available to a different selection principle.

Grouping the poems in the book being assembled is a particular instance of classification. There are likely to be various options, as (to take the bookcase analogy in an additional direction) there are in grouping the books on my shelves. Are they going to be in a single group, alphabetized by author? Will they be in groups by Dewey Decimal letter? Are they going to be arranged in groups by genre (poetry books on these shelves, novels over here...)? If so, will there be subgroups (poetry written in English here, poetry translated into English there; US poetry here, Canadian poetry here, Australian poetry here...)?

As with the books in my library, so with the poems in the book I'm assembling, there might be any number of groupings that would make good sense. And as with the books in my library, being deliberate about which basis I've settled on for the grouping of poems in my poetry book will be beneficial (even if that basis is intuition, rather than a rule). Either grouping my books by genre or by Dewey Decimal letter could make sense, but mixing the two would work less well. Analogously, there might be various ways to group my poems (love poems here and nature poems there; poems from last year here and poems from the year before there; etc.), but probably things will go best if I choose one way and stick with it: blurring those ways would be likely to prove less legible to a reader.

3. Sequence the poems.

In addition to selecting the poems for my book and grouping them, I will need to sequence them. In doing so, I will be answering the question, What carries the reader from one poem to the next? It is possible to select and apply an overarching principle that determines the sequence: I could choose to make my book an abecedarian, for example, or I could decide to arrange the poems chronologically by date of composition. It is also possible, though, and I take this as the more usual approach, to sequence poems on a more ad hoc basis, pair by pair: I've placed poem B immediately after poem A because A ends at sunset and B begins at sunrise, but I've situated poem C right after poem B because B depicts butterflies animating a buddleia bush and C depicts moths pestering a porch light.

As with the previous steps, so with the step of sequencing the poems in a book, no one basis is inherently or universally best. The world is a better place for having in it some abecedarians, but it wouldn't be made better if all poetry books were abecedarians. The question is what sequence works best for these poems in this book, and regarding decisions about sequence these instructions do not recommend any particular basis over others, only a particular attitude, namely that of performing the sequencing deliberately and reflectively. Which is only to reiterate that performing this step in assembling one's book, just like performing the other steps, is not mechanical but calls for judgment.

4. Arc the poems.

By arcing the poems, I mean answering, in the arrangement itself, the question What carries the reader from beginning to end? As noted above, arcing doesn't "pull apart" completely from sequencing, but they are not identical. Sequencing is the local or micro aspect of arranging the poems; arcing is the global or macro aspect. By analogy with following a map on a hike, sequencing is the point-by-point decision-making (first I have to ford this stream, then I'll cross a meadow...), and arcing is the point-to-point decision-making, when I'm standing at the trailhead, map in hand, looking over the terrain through which the trail winds (OK, so that's where we're headed).

Decisions about arcing might be variously related to principles for selection and sequencing. For instance, the selection principle of a year of COVID poems coordinates readily with arcing by chronology: the reader will be carried from the beginning of the book to its end by moving from the beginning of the year to its end. Or again, the sequencing principle of an abecedarian is also an arcing principle: it sequences the poems (I know to put my "N" poems after my "M" poems) and it carries the reader from the beginning of the alphabet to its end.

However they relate to the principles for selection and sequencing in a particular book, decisions about arcing will resemble decisions about selection and sequencing, in responding favorably to being made deliberately and in dependence on the judgment of the poet assembling the book.

5. Reconcile the poems.

Of the steps for book assembly enumerated here, this one would be the easiest to overlook, but performing it can add a level of refinement to the manuscript as a whole. Even poems that were conceived together (it was one idea, to write my numerous COVID poems) still get composed separately (I wrote my COVID poems one by one), and in the most typical case poems are published individually in journals before being collected in a book, so it is worth posing, to each poem in the book being assembled, the question, Does its presentation with other poems invite changes from this poem's freestanding version?

There may be many books for which the answer to the question is in every case no: each poem is unaffected by its new context and needs no revision before taking its place in the book. For such books, this step would be just a way of checking, making sure, and would not result in revision. It is easy, though, to imagine cases in which this step would bring changes. In a book whose poems feature a recurring character, for example, it might well be the case that a given poem in its freestanding, best-for-journal-publication form needed to include certain information about the character in order to make sense for the reader. If that information is given in other poems, it would be redundant in the given poems, and could be edited out. Something similar might hold for the individual poems in a book that is about a historical event or person: a given poem in its freestanding version might need to include some context or background that it could leave out in its collected version, if that context or background is given elsewhere in the book.

Even when no revision results, it is worth performing this step simply for confirmation.

6. Check your work.

Thinking of a poetry book in terms of its being, like a bookcase, parts assembled into a whole, offers as one benefit a clear ideal: to make the whole greater than the sum of its parts.

As with the instructions generally, there is a relevant difference here between bookcases and books. For the bookcase, the question is the whole greater than the sum of its parts? is a yes-or-no question that minimizes judgment. If the bookcase looks like the picture on the box, if it stands up and holds books, the answer is yes; if not, no. For the poetry book, things are more complex, and the question calls for judgment. The question admits of degree in regard to a poetry book in a way that it does not in regard to bookcases. Assembling the bookcase, I either did or didn't manage to make the whole greater than the sum of its parts: either it looks like the picture or it doesn't, either it holds books or it doesn't. Assembling the poetry book, though, I might arrive at one whole that is a little greater than the sum of its parts, and another that is a lot greater. There is not a given picture to compare it to and try to match. Still, making the whole greater than the sum of its parts remains the ideal.

In regard to the bookcase, the assembled whole does something—it holds books—that the sum of the parts (the parts as they arrived in the box, or as I laid them out on the rug prior to assembling them) does not. To add another analogy, a jigsaw puzzle, the whole (the assembled puzzle) shows something the sum of its parts (the pieces still in the box, or spread out on the dining room table) does not: a litter of kittens, the Portland Head Light, or whatever the picture is. That's what I'm aiming for, and thus what I'm checking for, in this step of the process of assembling my poems into a book: does the book do something or show something that the loose poems don't?

Options

I take it that the instructions as just outlined have a certain necessity and universality. Any poet, assembling any poetry book, in fact performs those steps. The benefit of explicitly stating them is not novelty (they don't show a new way to assemble a poetry book) or proprietariness ("Here's my way of putting a book together!"). The benefit is clarity, the sort that enables me to be more deliberate in assembling my book. In addition to those necessary steps, though, there are optional ones. I imagine that any poet who set out to make a list of assembly instructions would come up with one that looked a lot like the one just offered. The "standard features" of poetry book assembly are more or less uniform, but the "optional equipment" varies more. With that as my excuse for the quirkiness of the list, here are three optional instructions that I myself follow and find helpful.

1. Get physical.

I find it helpful, especially in regard to the first four steps above (selecting, sequencing, grouping, arcing), to make a tiny printout of the poems. I choose the option on my computer to print four pages per sheet, and then (manually, with scissors) cut out the poems, so that each is its own closely cropped card. That allows me to lay out the whole group of poems on a table or the floor and rearrange them at will. The physicality of this practice brings at least two benefits. First, it lets me see "the big picture" more clearly. My vision of the whole is (or at least seems!) clearer when I see the parts arrayed before me on the table than when I am "only" holding them in mind. And second, it lets me rearrange the pieces rapidly and easily. I can "shuffle" through more arrangements, faster, with my tiny cut-out poems than with larger, harder-to-manage, full-page print-outs.

I don't perceive this act of printing tiny versions of the poems and rearranging them as changing the outcome of the first four steps, so much as making the process easier and faster. It might not change, say, the sequence I finally settle on for the poems, but it certainly makes arriving at that sequence less arduous.

2. Get outside.

Another quirky practice that I myself value is to impose on a draft version of the book some "random" or "arbitrary" rule. As one example of such a rule, on more than one occasion I have applied, either to a subgroup of poems within a book, or to the whole book, the rule that I must pull a word from one poem and insert it somewhere into the next poem, replacing a word with the same number of syllables, then take the displaced word and insert it somewhere in the next poem, and so on throughout. As silly as this might seem at first, it is purposeful. I perceive it as offering a very important benefit: it repositions me in relation to the poems. It makes me, in some important sense, a listener to more than a speaker of the language, an attitude that I regard as valuable. I take this random-rule-imposition as a form of reverence, a way of performing deference to the wisdom contained in the language, recognizing and drawing on a wisdom that exceeds my own.

3. Get clear.

The traditional MFA in which I teach requires as part of each student's thesis an "artist statement" about the work; the low-residency MFA in which I teach requires of each student, prior to completing the thesis, a "craft essay" investigating a technique or aspect of craft. In my experience, both requirements consistently prove practical and very beneficial to students completing their theses (aka poets assembling their poetry books). To all my thesis advisees, I recommend directly applying the statement/ essay in a pass (or several passes) through a thesis draft (or drafts). If the craft essay was about, say, use of concrete nouns in preference to abstract nouns, then go through the draft, poem by poem, noun by noun, and look for opportunities to replace relatively abstract nouns with nouns that are more concrete. If the artist statement declares one's intention to rage against the machine, contesting the racist, misogynistic, homophobic, colonial premises that underlie the disastrous neoliberal global political and economic order by which humanity is currently oppressed, then go through the manuscript, poem by poem, checking to see that each does contest those premises, and does not inadvertently reinforce them.

Doing so offers at least two benefits. First, it is an effective heuristic. It focuses attention: instead of standing in the doorway to the living room, looking around idly, I'm purposefully hunting for the remote. I'm looking for something in the manuscript, and because my looking is directed, I notice things I wouldn't otherwise. Second, it is an effective diagnostic. It tests the poems against the poet's own ambitions and ideals for the work. In poetry as in other practices, it is easier to fulfill passively received ideals than to fulfill actively chosen ideals. It is easy to write what Adrienne Rich calls "the columnar, anecdotal, domestic poem, often with a three-stress line" when that is the going style, and easy to compose erasure poems when that is the fad. Expressly formulating what I value and what I want my poems to do, and then explicitly testing my poems against that ideal(s), at least pulls me in the direction of writing the poems I think I should be writing instead of the poems everyone else is writing.

Urging students toward this practice is not (merely) teacherly do-as-I-say advice: I find the practice very helpful in my own attempts to assemble poetry books. I mimic the process I recommend to others, writing out for myself an "artist statement" or "craft essay," and using it as a focus for a pass through a draft of the book.

Recap

Presentation here as a set of assembly instructions is meant to identify a set of salient considerations in putting together a poetry book: What poems should the book include? How should the poems be grouped? What carries the reader from one poem to the next? What carries the reader from beginning to end? Does its presentation with other poems invite changes from this poem's freestanding version? Is the whole greater than the sum of its parts?

These instructions can't make assembling a poetry book quite as simple and straightforward as assembling a store-bought bookcase from a kit, but I hope they do support its being similarly purposive and orderly.

Works Cited

Rich, Adrienne. "Defy the Space that Separates." *The Free Library.* 07 October 1996. https://www.thefreelibrary.com/Defy+the+space+that+separates.-a018717713. Accessed 19 May 2022.

Leaping Between Seams

What Analog Collage Taught Me About Sequencing a
Book of Poems

Karyna McGlynn

> *Our gaze has a reading speed of reality that cannot be transferred*
> *into a single image, except through the overlapping of multiple*
> *layers, moments and readings.*
> —Caterina Rossato, *Collage by Women: 50 Essential*
> *Contemporary Artists*

ONE OF MY most treasured childhood possessions was a book of paper dolls called *Glamorous Movie Stars of the Thirties*, featuring famous fashions of Joan Crawford, Jean Harlow, Greta Garbo—and my favorite, Judy Garland. I was a seven-year-old with shaky hands, a shitty pair of safety scissors, and no sense that there were other copies of this book in the world, so I allowed myself to cut out only one doll or outfit per month.

Every time was terrifying: navigating around intricate ruffles, fussy flowers, and wispy feathers. I had nightmares that I might sneeze and accidentally decapitate Carole Lombard. I made my mother take me to get each individual piece laminated at the Teacher Supply Store. Then I created little supper club scenarios for my starlets to parade around in their fantastical Erté gowns, their Irenes, their Heads, their Orry-Kellys.

These scenarios never looked as good in real life as they did in my head—certainly not glamorous enough for the likes of Joan Crawford, who sneered at me from the gluey shoebox speakeasy where I had posed her next to a goofy Ken Doll. It never once occurred to me to cut up my other books to bring my visions to life. And even if it had occurred to me, I would have dismissed it as something likely to get me in trouble. Over time, books started to overtake my room, all the pictures in them disappeared, and my laminated stable of screen goddesses got packed away.

• • •

I discovered art supply stores when I was a freshman at the University of Texas in the late '90s. I had no legitimate business being in these stores; I was an English major. I wasn't supposed to need anything beyond a used futon, a day-old bagel, or a random couplet tossed to the curb by some heartbroken philosophy minor on Sixth Street.

Still, I had this nagging feeling that in order to be a Real Artist I was supposed to be collecting something. I was born and raised in Austin. It's been an ascendant boomtown for my entire life. The accidental brilliance was abundant; you could just pick it out of the storm drains in the mornings like dumped ice—all swirled with sunrise & ripples of Chambord.

By that measure, art supply stores were exorbitantly expensive. I could neither afford nor justify making actual purchases. I was a poet; therefore, all the tools I would ever need were either free, abundant, abstract, or (god forbid) "inside me all along."

I understood instinctively that my chosen artform had no monetary value because it had no physicality, tangible tools, or price of admission. Any fool could be a poet, it seemed, just by declaring themselves to be one.[1]

---

1. Okay, so this isn't *entirely* true. How would I describe the Late '90s / Early 2000s Baby Poet Starter Kit?
   - $5 cash to get into The Poetry Slam.
   - Moleskine Notebook (Cover: bleached by sun. Elastic Strap: fatigued. Back Pocket: FULL).
   - Fat Fountain Pen (Usually a graduation gift from a grandpa. Requires special cartridges you won't ever be able to afford.)
   - Avery perforated "business" cards with swirly cappuccino-clip-art vibes (for all your Poetry Business).
   - Stuff for making chapbooks: Microsoft Publisher, cardstock, a saddle stapler, someone who can borrow their mom's minivan to drive you to Kinko's.
   - Distressed canvas messenger bag (for all the chapbooks you plan to sell at The Poetry Slam).

But no poet I knew could afford to buy natural modeling beeswax from Denmark.

The people who worked at art supply stores were *real* artists. You could just tell; they spoke softly, never smiled, and had intimidatingly large gauges in their ears, through which they would casually stick charcoal pencils, or joints, or little haikus about death.

I'd always wanted to be a visual artist, but I never showed any aptitude for drawing, painting, or sculpture, so I took up photography in my twenties, wandering the Seattle streets taking black-and-white shots of broken stilettos, apple blossoms in the gutter, lonely bus stops in the rain. Even years later, during my doctoral studies in literature, I would occasionally skip class to wander aspirationally through aisles of fancy art markers I somehow felt accused of stealing, or maybe even huffing. I ran my fingers over brushes, canvases, charcoals, modeling clay, bone folders, awls. "Medium-duty *awl*," I mouthed silently to myself, memorizing the words without knowing what to do with them. My very ignorance seemed to leave smudges on the handmade papers draped dramatically over wooden dowels. "*Dowel*," I mouthed. Sometimes, after lurking in the store for hours, I would buy a single Stabilo pen by way of apology before slumping away in embarrassment. What was I *looking* for?

• • •

I must have been trying to absorb the credibility that still (somehow) accompanies tangibility. Most poets wait years to see their poems become "tangible" in the form of a printed magazine or book. If you're brave/dumb enough to ever tell a stranger you're a poet, the stranger will inevitably ask, "Published??" Translation: "People Other than You and Your Parents were willing to use Real Ink & Real Paper to distribute Your Personal Musings to the General Public??"

I was presumably an artist; I was even a "Master of Fine Arts" (!). I'd spent half my life in workshops talking about the "craft" of the "trade" like

---

- Basic comprehension of Poet Math (e.g. If your chapbooks cost $12 each to make, but you sell them for $5 each because you're "not pretentious," how many copies must you sell in order to get you and your roommate into the Next Poetry Slam?)

some sort of medieval artisan's apprentice. At pubs across the Midwest, I'd gathered with fellow guildsmen! We'd huddle over pints at long wooden tables and speak deep into the night about the processes of sculpting our prose, stitching our scenes together, and scaffolding our poetic architecture. There was much talk about whether our underbaked ideas needed "more time in the oven." There were literal arguments about whether or not it was an insult for a poet-to-be described in a review as "skilled" or "painterly."

Suddenly there I was on the verge of becoming an actual "Doctor" (!). But where the hell were my tools? Where were my actual instruments to be able to demonstrate my expertise in anything?? It was all conceptual.

Art supplies are awesome because they are physical objects you can use to make physical objects that can depict different physical objects. They can be used to communicate emotional and spiritual complexity instantly, powerfully (often wordlessly), and to a casual passerby. I love poems a whole lot, but I've never met one that can do all that at once.[2]

• • •

And then I discovered collage.

And when I say *discovered*, I really mean it. Like in the etymologically Old French *descovrir* sense of the word. Like it was an existing Truth that was unveiled for me. It was right under the floorboards of my poetry, ticking like the Tell-Tale Heart. "Dissemble no more! I admit the deed! —tear up the planks! here, here!—It is the beating of my hideous heart!" Either way, it was (ugh) "inside me all along." I just needed a different set of materials to express it.

Discovering collage has been the ultimate realization of what I was trying to do with paper dolls as a child. Creating each canvas is like peering into the individual rooms of a giant dollhouse where I get to be both casting director and costume designer, makeup artist and location scout, lighting designer and director of photography.

As an adult, I'm only limited by what I can find and cut up without getting in trouble—which is to say basically unlimited. Thrift shops and

---

2. And this is why poet movies are always so boring: we're all just twiddling our pens like sad idiots in oversized cardigans, propping our feet on radiators in leaky English Departments, or slurping milky tea in window seats while the war rages around us.

library book sales are my jam. And despite my childhood frustration at not being able to create authentic replicas of Busby Berkley soundstages out of tinker toys, I know that the practice was instructive; figuring out how to make interesting juxtapositions out of the boring things in my bedroom was an early lesson in metaphor-making.

• • •

Poets are natural collagists.[3] We collect vivid images and cinematic scenes. We love repetition and variations on a theme. We live for interesting collisions. We collect the best textures we can find and we *weird* them. We understand shape and gesture. We fuss over detail work, move stuff around. We think about what the white space communicates. We think, "What can I cut? How can I compress? Have I milked the most interesting images?"

Poets instinctively seem to understand that the poem is not only utterance but *image*. And like visual artists, poets seem particularly interested in the question, "How much can I communicate in the space of a *single* frame or page?"

This is why we freak out when it comes to assembling a book: so many pages! We're used to thinking at a smaller scale. We're suddenly sure that none of our poems "go" with each other, like they're a pile of uselessly mismatched socks. But they're never nearly as mismatched as we think they are. The images, sounds, textures, and allusions in our poems may come from all over, but our *choices* about what to include and exclude speak their own language. That language is our aesthetic. It's the connective tissue that allows the random-ass bones of our poems to masquerade as a dancing skeleton.

Practicing collage has helped me form a more haptic vocabulary for thinking about my poetry—What's touching what? What does that proximity convey? Do these juxtapositions have energy? Do they imply move-

---

3. Tony Hoagland used to love to call us "skittery." This was more of an accusation than a compliment, I think. Though "skitteriness," like much of what Hoagland seemed to theatrically resent in poetry, was an art he'd also perfected. I mean, just look at a poem like "Requests for Toy Piano." It clatters and rolls its persnickety arpeggios around like two centipedes doing pleasure sprints in an old tin can!

ment? How do they change the depth of field? Do they transform? Have I allowed for some form of randomness to intervene?

While I'm not saying that poets need necessarily take up collage as a hobby, I do think it's important that we engage in some form of visual arts. This practice helps us better articulate our relationship to slippery concepts like aesthetic, style, tone, and (dear god) *voice*.

For instance, my poetic impulse and my collage aesthetic are virtually identical: theatrical, female-centric, drag-influenced, darkly humorous, decidedly maximalist—yet also obsessive about finding the geometry within the excess. Knowing this, when I feel blocked about some Poetry Problem (like the Prospect of, *ugh*, "Making a Book"), I collage. Surreal as collaging can be, it helps me Find Out What I Really Mean.[4]

• • •

When I think back to my Baby Poet days, I wasn't waiting on presses to recognize me; I was a one-woman chapbook factory. I was Putting Out Books. Sometimes I would release two in one month. Sometimes I swaddled them in vellum. One time I bound a Limited Run (lol) of a chapbook called *Turn Out* with the real ribbons from my old pointe shoes. Should I remain embarrassed by this?

Maybe the poetry wasn't always great, but my naivete made me bold and prolific. I would write a whole chapbook in a night or two, and have it printed and bound a week later. This is the sort of hyperactive and unselfconscious Beginner Brain that practicing collage helped me tap back into.

When I ask students what poetry they first fell in love with, the ones who are being honest say Lewis Carroll, Dr. Seuss, Maya Angelou, or Shel Silverstein—occasionally I get Cummings, Plath, or sometimes (excitingly!) a spoken word poet like Rudy Francisco, Anis Mojgani, or Andrea Gibson. Often someone will ask if I "count" these as poems. Most of my students are eighteen to twenty-three, but they've already been conditioned to believe that "real" poetry must be serious, pretentious, difficult, grim, and *dead*.

---

4. Nod to that Billy Collins poem "Introduction to Poetry" where all the students want to do is "tie the poem to a chair with rope / and torture a confession out of it. // They begin beating it with a hose to find out what it really means" (58).

Remember when you first fell in love with reading and writing poetry? Remember that sense of unlimited sonic terrain? The realization that you could stack image on top of image, sound on top of sound, and in those recombinations, create an *original* resonance? The thrill of new utterance! The plasticity of poetry—how it could expand or contract around any subject matter. The way poetry, like the TARDIS, was "bigger on the inside." The way a great metaphor might be waiting around the corner of any line. The way we learned to manipulate line breaks to control the flow of sensory data. The way we learned that each word, line, and stanza is a unit that can be cut, copied, moved, ripped, pasted, erased, colored, or mixed. The way the poem uses juxtaposition and compression to peek through the windows of disparate realities. And the way poetry embraces absurdity—the way a good poem always keeps at least a few tendrils in the psychedelic dream-logic of early childhood. These are things Max Ernst always understood. While he had no formal training, Ernst was a prolific surrealist and Dadaist artist: an accomplished poet, collagist, painter, sculptor, and graphic designer. Ernst also invented several collage-adjacent art techniques (including frottage and grattage) and is credited with creating what many consider the first graphic novel, *Une semaine de bonté* (*A Week of Kindness*), an epic work of surrealist storytelling through collage.[5]

"Creativity," Ernst once remarked, "is that marvelous capacity to grasp mutually distinct realities and draw a spark from their juxtaposition" (Ernst as qtd by Fabun 6). That might as well be the definition of poetry, yet every poet I know is convinced that they are uniquely unqualified to organize a poetry manuscript.

It's no surprise we fear this part of the process. Imposter syndrome is practically a prerequisite for being a poet, and nothing inflames our imposter syndrome quite like the prospect of conceptualizing and organizing an entire book.[6] By the time we get to the stage where we're "seriously"

---

5. I first encountered *Une semaine de bonté* as an undergrad, and it had such a profound aesthetic effect on me, that I've basically been writing a book-length ekphrastic response to it ever since. I think one of things that first impressed me about Ernst's art was the way he could *hide the seams* of his components while still *emphasizing their contrast*. The results are uncanny. They look like a long-ago dream that you only just now remembered.
6. With, like, primary and secondary themes? And an arc?! And a rationale that we can stomach hearing ourselves reiterate to anyone willing—or naive enough—to listen?! And

constructing a full-length book of poetry, many of us seize up. "Playtime is *over*," we think. "Now I have to prove to the world that I Have Something Important to Say."

• • •

For the final project in my poetry workshops, I ask students to create chapbooks. They are responsible for all aspects of production: writing, editing, layout, design, cover art, paper choice, printing, and binding. On the last week, they give readings from their chapbooks. Initially, they balk at the task. They think they won't be able to do it, but they almost always can—often brilliantly. I show them tons of examples from previous students—some hand-painted, some sewn or quilted, one bound with bolts and nuts, another that unfolds like a bilingual accordion from a black velvet box. When they show up with their chapbooks in their backpacks, some are glowing.[7]

I know that glow. It's the glow of making your aesthetic *tangible*. And you don't even have to make a whole chapbook to experience it. I highly recommend trying to design your own book cover.[8] This practice will not only help you better articulate your aesthetic, but also help you assess your title and your target audience in visual terms. Use any medium or set of skills/tools that speak to you. I think you should try collage, but I'm obviously biased.

• • •

In the corners of #collage Instagram where I hang out, process videos are super popular. It's exactly what it sounds like: a time-lapse video of an analog collage in the process of being made. My favorite ones show the collagist trying out the same cut-out image—say, a plummeting Icarus—on a bunch of different backgrounds in rapid succession.

---

a title that brands our book and us as a particular sort of thing forever and ever?! And what if it's all a lie and nobody has bothered to disabuse us of the notion that we're writers for all this time because it's just too awkward?

7. The students, that is. Though I've admittedly received a couple of glow-in-the-dark chapbooks!

8. Just as an experiment. I don't actually recommend submitting your poetry manuscript with preexisting visual art attached as a condition of publication.

The possibilities flash before us: Icarus plummeting into a gator's mouth, or into Saturn's rings, or a bed of snoozing puppies—so many tempting options! How will she ever choose?? And suddenly, there it is: the combo she can't look away from. The one where the borders of the pieces seem to dissolve into each other and speak a new language—the one where Icarus might fall out of the sea and into the sky of his father's forgiveness.

There's an inherent playfulness that accompanies collage-making: Why *not* show a tiger leaping from a volcano? And why *not* replace the rim of the volcano with the coral-lipsticked mouth of a screaming woman? And while we're at it, why not go ahead and let Jesus surf down the lava flow into the hungry arms of hundreds of wild Elvis fans? These sorts of low-stakes, humorous juxtapositions are a hallmark of collage's origins in Surrealism. We bring this understanding to the act of collaging. We sit down amidst our textures/toys, and the inner child instinctively understands: it's playtime. I think these collage process videos should be required viewing for any poet currently assembling a manuscript. Is the process of sequencing a poetry manuscript much different??

As a collagist, my biggest bursts of creative activity reliably follow epic cutting sessions. I do my best collages when I have a surfeit of "fresh cuts." As I'm cutting out an image—a robot arm from *NatGeo*, let's say—my brain is already busy making connections—imagining evocative juxtapositions and potential color palettes. Sometimes chance works in my favor; like, maybe when I toss the robot arm into the pile of fresh cuts, it lands next to a large conch shell. Now the robot arm emerges from the shell like the tendril of a futuristic mollusk!

Maybe it's silly, but collaging has helped me rediscover the jouissance that brought me to poetry in the first place—the aspects that made it feel more like magic than like work. Don't forget: your book-in-progress is full of futuristic mollusk tendrils. The patterns are there; you just have to prioritize some play time to find them.

Initially, any big art project seems like an impossible task—vast in scope and requiring some sort of abject devotion at the altar of aesthetic obsession. But when you start breaking the project down into workable components—sections, scenes, squares, quadrants, days, acts, stanzas, steps—it feels way friendlier. I'm all about keeping it friendly.

Remember, you already know how to do this.

• • •

Turning Your "Chaos" into a Concept

1. **Begin from a place of abundance.** This means having *more* poems than you need. Full-length poetry collections are usually between forty-eight and eighty pages, but don't make the mistake of trying to wrangle the first forty-eight pages of poetry you have into a book. Instead, give yourself plenty of material to pick and choose from. I recommend having at *least* seventy pages of poetry to work with. If you don't have that yet, go write some more poems before continuing with the second step.[9]

2. **Set yourself up for greatness.** You need a solid chunk of time to devote to this. Put it on your calendar. Consider set and setting. Find an area to spread out that's free of traffic/distractions. Make your space conducive to Art Magic (e.g. straighten up, light some candles, put on a Cocteau Twins album or something).

3. **Prime your "canvas."** In preparation for assembling your manuscript, do the following:

    a. Find two recent poetry collections you love. Read them quickly, and with an eye toward structure. How do the poets you admire organize *their* material? The structure is often a bit looser than you might imagine, which is freeing!

    b. Quickly write a new poem to limber up your associative skills. (Don't overthink this; it's probably not going in your manuscript.)

4. **Print out all the potential good stuff.** You *know* what your good stuff is. Shut up. Yes, you do. If you have any promising in-progress poems, go ahead and print those pieces as well. Don't worry about whether any of it "goes together" yet. Remember: your aesthetic is the glue that will bring disparate pieces *together*.

---

9. You *like* writing poems, remember??

5. **Spread out the "chaos" on the floor.** When it comes to fully conceptualizing creative projects, there's no substitute for getting down on the floor and strategically spreading stuff out. This is not some generation-specific affectation; it's actually super useful for envisioning the macrostructure and flow of many creative projects in a way that you can't effectively replicate on your devices. Get a bird's-eye view. These are no longer Your Precious Poems; they are *materials*, and they all have the potential to become components of a larger structure.

6. **Use keywords & color-coding.** Grab some pens/markers/pencils in a variety of colors. *Very* quickly read through your pieces, writing bullet-point keywords on each page as you go. Key words might include prominent themes, topics, images, colors, locations, time periods, POVs, formal attributes, editorial comments, and stylistic characteristics.

Here's an example of real keywords I wrote on a poem I'm currently trying to work into a manuscript:

- Narrative second person POV
- Long lines (stylistic outlier?)
- Lush, sonic, obsessive, baroque, serious, scary, feminist
- Cold, dark, water, ice
- Adolescence, cars, music, recklessness, abusive/controlling boyfriends, mania, near-death experiences

I then color-coded the upper right-hand corner of the piece with long, wavy, black-and-blue lines (a visual shorthand signaling this poem is cold, watery, dark, long-lined, and intense).

In the process of training your attention in this way, some pretty interesting patterns should reliably begin suggesting themselves.

7. **Create a working armature or scaffolding.** Pull aside the pieces that (for whatever reasons) feel *most fundamental* to this book (like, you can't even *imagine* your book without them). Consider how each of these poems might function architecturally. If there are multiple pieces, perhaps they suggest sections, or strands in a braid. If you have a long poem or sequence, could you use that as a centerpiece to spiral out from?

You might also start forming stacks or constellations of poems using your keywords / color-coding as guides. When I'm collaging, I often start by grouping my cuts by color, size, texture, theme (e.g. this is the "sorbet sunset" stack, and this is the box "where all the tiny people go," and these are my twin stacks of portals / whirlpools & paths / planks). I invite you to employ such nonsense when making a book, and also whenever you want.

8. **Consider: What's the *first* line the reader should read? And what's the *last* line the reader should read?** Awesome. These are your first and last poems. You can think of them as bookends that your book must bridge. Your *only* goal now is to get the readers across that bridge. Consider how your organization might help them make a *safe*, *scenic* and *satisfying* journey[10] from one end to the other.

9. **As you sequence, pay special attention to the "seams."[11]** Underline the all-important first and last lines of each piece. Along with your poem and section titles, these first and last lines are the "seams" (i.e. the segues between one piece and the next—or, the places where you have the opportunity to stitch individual materials into the "quilt" of the whole and make it seem like you had a plan all along).

You know how in a crown of sonnets you're supposed to repeat the last line of each sonnet in the first line of the succeeding sonnet? Well, we're using a similar technique here... only, we're trying to identify preexisting repeating elements that will create the illusion of moving seamlessly from one poem to the next. Look for places where the seams between pieces seem to dissolve into each other. Let your mind "squint" a bit. Look for patterns, repetitions, and resonances—anything that might link the end of one piece with the beginning of another.

You can see this sequencing technique at play all over my books. Here are a few examples from *Hothouse*:

---

10. I simply *cannot* be trusted with alliteration. I'm so sorry.

11. Don't you think so much of art is about learning to manipulate the seams and joins? The weak points that threaten to betray the vulnerability of our art, the "made-ness" of it, the cringey parts that threaten to explode in the kiln. Whenever you clumsily force a line of poetry, or ham-fistedly juxtapose a "sacred" image with a "profane" one, aren't you uncomfortably aware of the way you have somehow "betrayed the seam"?

a. The first poem in the "Library" section, "Russel Says
    Everybody is Aubrey" ends with the line "R picks up D's
    books one by one, renaming them Aubrey." Fittingly, the
    next poem is called "Our Books, Our Books." It begins
    with the line, "The question is whether to quell this
    profligate book writing" and ends with the phrase "If Love
    is the sicker of two sick, / sick puppies, what choice do we
    have? / We must bring it home and fix it." The following
    poem is called "Caretaker" and begins with the line, "I'm
    in charge of this mustard brown vase and so far / I'm not
    doing a very good job."

b. The first poem in the "Basement" section, "Rich Girl
    Camp Revenge Fantasy" concludes with an image of class
    conflict: "You're up in the branches clutching a pitcher /
    of barbecue sauce. Below, our parents snake / through the
    oaks in a line of seersucker / & clean, white Suburbans."
    The next poem, "Fortune is a Woman in Furs at the Food
    Bank," begins with an image of class conflict and
    concludes with the line "Just to show them a thing or two
    about luxury." The next poem, "Elegiac Stanzas (with
    Rhinestones)," begins by invoking luxury, class conflict
    and death: "Let me tell you how Princess Di died for me."
    [The poem's speaker, we discover, is working at a strip club
    called The Palace.] It concludes with Princess Di's death:
    "and the manager, against his wishes, / had to shut down
    the Palace and send / his inconsolable princesses home."
    The next poem is, of course, called "Of all the Dead People
    I Know" (etc.).

I include the above not to bore you with the minutiae of my book, but
to practically illustrate my point about looking for the places where the
seams "speak" to each other. Once you get the hang of this technique it
will feel almost like cheating (!) because it will make your sequence seem
super intentional—as if you wrote all the poems in the order they appear.

I didn't write *any* of the poems in *Hothouse* as a sequence. As far as I
was concerned, they were all "mismatched sock" poems (a belief which

kept me from completing that book for a really long time). But they weren't mismatched at all. Because I'm me. And because these poems are products of a specific time / place / generation / literary aesthetic. And because I'm a Scorpio/Leo who (duh) loves talking about Art, Sex, Death, Class, Performance, and Gender. Because my work—like your work—constellates around the same clusters of thematic and stylistic stars. You may be the last one to recognize it, but trust me: you have an aesthetic. It will shine through—especially if you *try* to write the thing you *wish* you were reading.

10. **Now, be like the bowerbird!** Commit to a colorway and execute your concept with Ruthless Beauty! Woo your viewers with exciting shapes and textures! Sure, it's an illusion, but what isn't?? If you're seriously reading essays right now about how to make a poetry book, then you've already chosen some kind of eclectic lifepath. Lean *way* into that part of you during this entire process. That's the only way to make a book. Don't bore the muses. Be both bold and humble. Ask for help when you need it. Be grateful and considerate when you get it. Always be willing to edit. Also know when to stop.[12]

• • •

In school I studied under a handful of old hippie poets who had the whiff of Naropa about them. They wore the type of vests and braided leather bracelets that can only be bought off a blanket. In their psychedelic beneficence, they always tried to steer our workshops into deep, metaphysical waters: "Is this a poem, or is it…an invocation?" "We could discuss this poem…or…we could discuss the demons hiding under the frilly bedding of this poem's self-consciousness."

We played along because these poetry shamans were "poetry famous," and also because they were brilliant. They'd read everything. They were sage and unshockable. They beckoned us toward nature and self-knowledge,

---

12. You're only procrastinating because finishing this book means staring into the Existential Abyss of the "next" one. But, um, remember when Ed Harris dove into the abyss in the 1989 movie *The Abyss*?? What he found down there was cool AF and, frankly, should have been elaborated upon further. This is just to say: finish your dang book. Don't you want to be free to explore again?

waved us away from cynicism and careerism. This didn't make sense to us. These poetry shamans had tenure-track positions at major universities. Who were they to lecture us about "writing less and walking more" when they were already sitting pretty in the ivory tower, eating exotic fruits and licking the juice from their elfin fingers?

At the bar after workshops, we drank strong ales, squinted through thick eyeliner, and bitched about how they weren't "even helping us" with our books. We danced to Interpol and Amy Winehouse. We chain-smoked through our side parts, had casually careerist hookups, dubbed everything "dubious," and were always "freaking out" about our manuscripts.

But it's not that they weren't *trying* to help us with our books; it's just that we didn't like how they were doing it.

They gave advice, but it was often epigrammatic, Dada-inflected, or downright chaotic. For example, when one of my classmates asked about "practical strategies" for sequencing her poetry manuscript, the professor answered her question with a question: "Have you ever considered abandoning your book-baby to the haphazard whims of fate by just tossing it down the stairs?" The student blinked; what could she say? The professor continued: "Have you ever considered just *asking* the book what order it wants to be in? How do you know it won't *answer* you?" Was this fool joking? We couldn't tell. It was infuriating.

Hilariously, I now love these strategies. And I understand what the professor was getting at: we had gotten too serious about *poetry*, of all things. We needed to reintroduce playfulness, surprise, and even a bit of magic.

• • •

Stop telling yourself these weird stories about how you're "bad" at sequencing / structure. Or how you "suck at titles / endings."

Poets are great at this stuff: form, compression, memorable lines. The associative leaping you instinctively employ as a poet (via imagery, enjambment, metaphor, etc.) is the same skill set you should tap into when it comes to sequencing. How do you organize a single poem, and how might you scale that organization up to a full manuscript?

In Robert Bly's essay "Looking for Dragon Smoke," he describes the best ancient art as having at its center "a long floating leap…a leap from the conscious to the unconscious and back again, a leap from the known part of the mind to the unknown part and back to the known" (1). For Bly, this leaping is the "real joy of poetry" (4). He argues that "leaping" is about ecstatic association, or heightened metaphor making:

> Thought of in terms of language, then, leaping is the ability to associate fast. In a great ancient or modern poem, the considerable distance between the associations, the distance that spark has to leap, gives the lines their bottomless feeling, their space, and the speed of association increases the excitement of the poetry. (4)

This (!). *This* is the stuff that quickens your pulse when you're in Poetry Flow State.

This is the source you draw on every time you reach for at simile, or meaningfully enjamb a line, or consider the spot where the poem must turn. This is the source you must trust now. Let it radiate out to the question, "Where must the *page* turn?" And then (if applicable): "Where must the *section* begin?" Finally: "Where must the *book* end?"

This is the source that will recognize a Last Line—in a dense crowd—immediately.

Works Cited

Bly, Robert. "Looking for Dragon Smoke." *Leaping Poetry: An Idea with Poems and Translations*. University of Pittsburgh Press, 2008, pp. 1–6.

Collins, Billy. "Introduction to Poetry." *The Apple that Astonished Paris*. University of Arkansas Press, 1988, p. 58.

Ernst, Max. *Une semaine de bonté: A Surrealistic Novel in Collage*. Dover Publications, 1976.

Fabun, Don. *You and Creativity*. Collier-MacMillian, 1969.

Hoagland, Tony. "Requests for Toy Piano." *Unincorporated Persons in the Late Honda Dynasty*. Graywolf Press, 2010, p. 61.

McGlynn, Karyna. Excerpted lines from *Hothouse*, Sarabande Books, 2017.

Poe, Edgar Allan, Arthur Hobson Quinn, and Edward Hayes O'Neill. *The Complete Tales and Poems of Edgar Allan Poe: With Selections from His Critical Writings*. Barnes & Noble, 1992.

Rossato, Caterina. "Caterina Rossato." *Collage by Women: 50 Essential Contemporary Artists*, edited by Rebeka Elizegi. Promopress, 2019, pp. 50–53.

Dreaming the Total Poem, Assembling the Counterarchive, Writing the Refuge

Philip Metres

A BOOK IS a talisman, a paper shield, a magic portal, a counterarchive, a momentary refuge. Even in the age of mechanical reproduction and digital self-publication, a book still feels more than a language delivery system, with its mysteries and hundreds of bound wings. So many of us—even those whose reading is rare or limited to little screens—still carry the word "book" in their mouths with a kind of reverence, a line item on the aspirational human bucket list.

When I first began writing, I saw literature as a country, a possible homeland, scattered between bindings. I suppose most of us who turn to writing have this nagging feeling that the lands available—in the world and on the page—have not quite space enough for our habitation, and so we set out to build my own little linguistic patch of a country.

The idea of a book, its totemic monumental solidity, sometimes puts into shadow the millions of intricate moves that make up a collection of poems. A first book of poems—like any hard-won first—seems like an impossible green light toward which we row, like Gatsby, against the current of time and necessity and sometimes our own self-sabotage.

Robert Frost once said that if a book has twenty-four poems, the book itself is the twenty-fifth. A book is more than the sum of its parts. The mystery for the writer to solve is: what is that twenty-fifth poem? Through-out the process of building the book, that twenty-fifth poem begins to take shape. The title, the cover image, the table of contents—all the para-text—offers a bit of that poem, but the twenty-fifth poem is more than the paratext. Often, we don't know until nearly the end the final stanzas of that poem, though increasingly—with the birth of the so-called "project book," where the entire book has a singular, unified subject and struc-ture—poets write toward that twenty-fifth poem from the start.

Neil Friastat calls the twenty-fifth poem the "contexture" of the book—the "contextuality provided for each poem by the larger frame within which it is placed, and the resultant texture of resonance and meanings" (13). Alberto Ríos offers nineteen separate but overlapping organizing strategies:

1. temporal narrative
2. backward temporal
3. character growth
4. convergent narrative
5. the trip
6. nature
7. organic
8. link by motif
9. thematic
10. orchestrated
11. idea
12. logical
13. spiral structure
14. mosaic
15. objective
16. alphabetical
17. eccentric
18. last-line/first-line dialogue (like a crown)
19. the "old neighborhood."

Some of these are self-evident and often boring ways to organize a book (hat tip to linear narrative, idea, and theme), but others—like orchestrated, spiral, backward temporal, convergent narrative—offer new ways of creating an architecture where all the individual poems are weight-bearing necessities.

Looking back at my own journeys of putting four books together, I can see elements of these approaches and structures. Here's a jaunt by them, waving at their chaos.

After more than a dozen years of writing poems, I completed my MFA and started sending around *A House Without*. Over the course of six years, in which it was a finalist for book contests twenty-four times, the manuscript would change from *A House Without* to *Ashberries* to *Echolocation Islands*, and finally to *To See the Earth*, with encouragement from then-Cleveland State University Poetry Center director Michael Dumanis. The title itself seemed to go through a process of expansion and contraction—from a house, to berries, to islands, to the whole earth. (The original title still feels like a secret poetics statement.)

What writing poetry has taught me is to engage in the dance of expansion and contraction, a dance with many rounds. I long for poems that seethe and breathe multitudes, but whose forms have the tensility and intricacy of webs. The same principle applies for sequences and collections of poems.

A chapbook comprised of most of the poems from the first section of that book—*Primer for Non-Native Speakers*—was published in 2004, slaking my desire to have something to share at readings, and giving me encouragement to keep trying, despite the grim record of rejections. Publishing a chapbook as a stepping-stone toward the island of a full-length collection has followed for most of my poetry books. Invariably, that step offered me another chance to revise the work, and let go what seemed extraneous to the larger work.

The basic form of *To See the Earth* was—after an initial ars poetica—three sections, each of which had its own geography: Russia, (immigrant) family, and wider and wider peregrinations. *To See the Earth* travels to Russia, memorializes immigrant Arab American family life in a Brooklyn brownstone, witnesses the violence visited upon people both at home and abroad, and carves out of such losses images of hope—the birthing not of a terrible beauty, but of the "dreaming disarmed body." I had become obsessed with what Fredric Jameson called "cognitive mapping"—a kind of "situational representation on the part of the individual subject to the vaster and properly unrepresentable totality" (51). To phrase this more simply: I was longing to belong, to understand how I belonged to myself and to others, to the places I had found and lost myself in this interconnected yet impossibly complex world.

Why did I structure it this way, beginning with my year living in Russia, rather than poems about family—which, chronologically, occurred prior to that year? I can see now that I wanted to unhouse the reader as I was unhoused, cast into an alien land. That year was so life-altering for me that it made sense to begin there. (A person leaves home is, after all, one of the most elemental of stories.) Those poems also stood out, no doubt, amid the many collections that might begin with coming-of-age autobiographical poems.

I began writing the poems that would comprise *Sand Opera* long before *To See the Earth* came out. The neat chronology of writing one book— completing and publishing it, and then writing another—has never worked for me, because I like to have multiple pots on the creative stove, and because I don't have the privilege of a press tapping its foot, waiting impatiently for the next thing.

Sand Opera emerged from a desire to write back against the trauma of the Abu Ghraib prison scandal, which broke in early 2004. The *abu ghraib arias* emerged from a crisis of representation; at some point, after poring over the photographs taken by US military police at Abu Ghraib of tortured prisoners, I decided that I could not write my way into or out of them. To continue to circulate the photographs themselves would only complete the total objectification of the bodies and souls of tortured Iraqis. It was only when I stumbled on transcripts of the testimony given by the Iraqi prisoners themselves did I discover a way to slip inside that prison. Whitman's phrase, "through me many long dumb voices," captures something of my method—because it seems to contain both the derisive silencing of those the society perceives as inhuman and the sense of their prolonged muteness. How victims are always doubly victimized when they aren't heard or lose the authority to speak. The aria poems began as a way to read the testimonies of the tortured at Abu Ghraib, which were too painful for me to read straight through. The only way I could bear to read them was to work with them, to see words and phrases vibrate on the page and to choose them, to bear down with them, to speak them—so as not to be overwhelmed by them.

The *arias* began as a witness to the voices of the prisoners, but the poem found its other half when I began to work with the language of the Standard Operating Procedure manual and words from various US military personnel who served at the Abu Ghraib prison. Before that, I'd focused entirely on the language of the Iraqi prisoners, which was the big aporia in the mainstream narrative of Abu Ghraib; yet I wanted to pull back a little, as in that photograph from the Abu Ghraib scandal where Ivan Frederick is visible looking down the image captured in a silver camera cradled in his hands, in the foreground of the picture where the infamous picture of the hooded detainee is standing on a box with wires attached to his hands and feet. The poems of victims and perpetrators were like two sides of the brain in the same skull. The leaping between these hemispheres, I hope, sutures together the testimony/cries of the tortured and the logics of the soldiers—some of whom participated in the torture, and some of whom tried to end it. I wanted to represent a range of responses by soldiers: the witnesses, the rationalizers, the complicit, the sadists, and the whistleblowers (such as Joe Darby).

That was the beginning. Once *abu ghraib arias* was complete (and became a chapbook published in 2011), I wanted to avoid staying in that prison, the prison of Abu Ghraib and the prison of misprision, of seeing Iraqis as victims only. The title *Sand Opera* came quite early—by 2009— an erasure of the longer (secret) title, revealed on the title page, Standard Operating Procedure. In the early 2000s, WikiLeaks released the Standard Operating Procedure manual for the Guantanamo Bay prison. What I discovered was a dry document of protocols for running a detention facility; but in some of its details, it demonstrated a remarkable amount of cultural sensitivity—about how to handle a Qur'an properly, and more ominously, how to conduct a proper Muslim burial. The fact that this was the place where Qur'ans would be thrown in the toilet and men forcibly smeared in the face with menstrual blood suggests the agonizing dissonance between US law (and cultural knowledge) and the conduct of military intelligence and CIA in the war on terror.

As *Sand Opera* continued to take shape, I realized that I hadn't really written about my own life. I was documenting, witnessing, and imagining, but I wasn't standing on my own ground, in my own experience. I thought about how strange it was that the very impetus for my identification with the Iraqi prisoners, the context for my wanting to reach out to them in some way through language, the fact of my Arab American background and experience, was not made explicit. That's where the prose/sonnet cells "On the flight overseas" emerged, meditations about being Arab American after 9/11. And "hung lyres," about my experience as a father absorbing this war through my daughter's absorption of it, asking me questions about refugees, and amputees, and suicide bombings. I'd listen to the radio surreptitiously rather than openly, arguing with NPR and their pronunciations and analyses, which my daughter, as all children do, absorbed as well: "It's ear rock, not eye rack," as she once said to some journalist on the radio. So I began with witnessing the other, but then I had to return to myself. I've had to try to figure out how to speak my own truth. How to be comfortable within my own skin. But even just writing those poems was a way of making my life more visible and real to myself.

In the process of reading and trying to make sense of how the war on terror was being conducted abroad, I learned about the use of "black sites"— secret prisons for interrogation. The story of Mohamed Farag Ahmad Bashmilah struck me with force, partly because it included renderings of drawings that Bashmilah had made while in various black sites around the world—in order to make sense of where he was and what was happening to him. I wanted to include Bashmilah's version of those spaces, in all their painstaking detail (right down to the broken-down, Russian-made jeep outside one compound). His testimony, taken from the legal case against Jeppesen Dataplan for its complicity in shuttling secret prisoners for the CIA, is full of such stunning detail—about the scar on the doctor who examined him, the Rubik's Cube he was given, the plastic water bottles that revealed what country he was in, the sounds of voices beyond the compound wall—that I wanted his longing to appear in some proximity to the solid walls of imprisonment. (The original story about Bashmilah, appearing online in *Salon* in 2007, was stripped of its images for reasons I never could find out, which made it even more important to share them.)

At first, Bashmilah's drawings were embedded inside the poetic sequence, "Homefront/Removes." But a friend suggested that I liberate those drawings from their direct counterpart, and spread them throughout the book. These strange drawings, enhanced by the publisher's use of vellum overlays, added a sense of mystery and disjuncture to the book as a whole. They became a kind of secret fascia that held together the layers of the body of the book. Mark Nowak's *Shut Up Shut Down* and *Coal Mountain Elementary*, each of which braided poems and photographs, encouraged me to experiment with photographs and drawings. Placing an image of Saddam Hussein's fingerprints, taken by the military, alongside a love poem that ends with a reference to hands, dizzied me—that surprise for the writer that Frost suggests might surprise the reader as well.

Sand Opera employs the tropes of opera in its structure and themes. The book's sections, as in classic opera, reference both "arias" and "recitatives," the two dominant modes of opera, roughly corresponding to lyric and narrative/dramatic modes in poetry, and that structural device actively guided choices about how the work moved between aria and recitative. Having the title helped me to visualize and pattern the kinds of rising and falling that might take place in an actual opera.

In the final stages of the work, I considered what sort of statement *Sand Opera* was making about the Iraq War as a whole, and about Iraq itself. I wanted to avoid war-writing clichés, in which others are depicted as monsters or martyrs. Later poems like "A Toast (for Nawal Nasrallah)" anchored the book in intimate friendships. Though the book began as a post-9/11 attempt to intervene on the conduct of the war, it ended up becoming history when the book came out in 2015. This lag of creation makes me value work that doesn't depend too heavily on a contemporary moment, but has its taproot in some persistence, some ongoing flowing vitality.

My third book, *Pictures at an Exhibition: A Petersburg Album*, was inspired by a residency in St. Petersburg for the Summer Literary Seminar in 2002, precisely a decade after I'd lived in Russia. During a workshop, Kim Addonizio gave us an assignment to keep an image notebook of our time in that spectacle of a city. I had no idea what to do with these images— these images that weren't just images, but palimpsests of images from the present to my previous times in the city, to all the historical layers that announce themselves in Petersburg.

That is, until I listened again to Modest Musorgsky. His "Pictures at an Exhibition" provided a scaffolding to order the chaos of images. I reshuffled, reordered, and organized the images and mini-poems to rhyme with the incredible piece of music. Scored to the movements of Mussorgsky's legendary modern suite—a work of art elegizing a lost friend, the artist Hartmann—*Pictures* takes the reader on a guided tour of this imperial city. The titles of poems riff on titles from Musorgsky's "Pictures," and attempt to render in language something of their spirit. For example, the second movement, "Gnomus" (Gnome), has been described as "a sketch depicting a little gnome, clumsily running with crooked legs" whose "lurching music, in contrasting tempos with frequent stops and starts, suggests the movements of the gnome." My poetic rendering includes three poems meditating on the poetics of deformity. The book, then, becomes a double-dialogue with a work of art and with the images of life.

Finally, a header and footer poem frame the entire sequence, summoning the ghost of a photographic album. The header poem was inspired by the fact that everywhere I went in St. Petersburg, I saw buildings covered by scaffolds and green curtains, inside of which workers were doing the renovations for three-hundredth anniversary of the city. In a book that is firmly a travelogue, I still wanted the book to make visible the material realities of these workers, many of them non-Russian immigrants, doing incredibly dangerous jobs. The footer poem is an *aide-mémoire*, which recounts my earlier time in the city. I had never seen a book of poems have running headers and footers before, and I spent an enormous amount of time thinking about how the headers and footers might rhyme with each page. I had to work with the manuscript in pre-typeset format, to approximate where page breaks might occur, in order to thread everything together.

Writing *Shrapnel Maps*, my fourth book, concerns the predicament of Palestine and Israel. If in *Sand Opera*, I felt overcome by the language of testimony and trying to keep my head above its waters, in *Shrapnel Maps*, I felt as if I were already far underwater, seeking the end of water in the shimmering light above my head. I knew something of the grand narratives of Palestine and Israel, but I knew how little I knew about what it might feel like to be inside and outside of the structures of power.

As a poet working with documentary evidence and the archive, I want to learn something, not to prove something, I want to be opened again to what the document shows and cannot show—and to create a space where a reader might encounter that directly. In this way, it's like writing every other poem, moving between a resolute tenacity in your vision and a nimble openness to what you cannot yet see, and trust that you will know when your tenacity should give way to flexibility, and when your will should cede to the poem's will. Take, for example, "Ark In," my blackout of a page of Mark Twain's *Innocents Abroad*.

Instead of merely ironizing a canonical (and also Orientalist and racist) literary text—a typical strategy of erasure or blackout poetry—I discovered that Twain himself was concerned with the problem of Orientalist representations, and the need to "unlearn" all the stereotypes that he'd inherited, and the problem of "a system of reduction." It struck me with force that knowing the problem doesn't mean that one will not replicate it. Having this note in the book, in the wider contrapuntal music of the work, is a reminder to author and reader of every work's limits.

Once I knew that Copper Canyon was open to a book with full color visuals, I began working to scatter images around each sequence. Many of them were renderings (or cropped versions of) "Visit Palestine" posters, originally made by Mitchell Loeb for the Tourist Office of the Jewish Agency for Palestine in 1947. I was astonished by these posters, which I discovered in a number of places online as I was researching the representations of Palestine particularly during the British Mandatory period (1920–1947). I found it intriguing how they appeared on both Palestinian sites—trying to reclaim the name Palestine—and Israeli sites, as vintage culture. The images of the place are stylized projections of the land, as Orientalist as you can imagine—they sometimes look like Iowa, sometimes like "the Orient." Working with Photoshop, I engaged in my own croppings and erasures, becoming a kind of ghost archive, alongside the other images and the poems.

Overall, *Shrapnel Maps* is organized variously—by the dialogical, temporal, and geographical. First, the order enacts a dialogic impulse, insofar

MARK ~~TWAIN~~

~~No man can stand here merely deserted Air Mellichab~~
~~and say the prophecy has not been fulfilled.~~
~~Every verse from the Bible which I have quoted~~
~~harry occurs the phrase "all these kings." It at~~
~~tracted my attention in a moment, because it carries~~
~~~~ a vastly different ~~significance from~~
~~what it always did at~~ home. I can see easily ~~enough~~
~~that if I wish to profit by this tour and come to a~~
~~sound understanding of the matters of interest~~
~~connected with it,~~ I must ~~studiously and faithfully~~
unlearn a great many things ~~I have somehow ac~~
~~quired~~ concerning Palestine. I must begin a system
of reduction. ~~Like my grapes which the spies bore~~
out of ~~the Promised Land, I have got everything~~
~~in Palestine on too large a scale. Some of my~~
~~ideas were wild enough. The word Palestine always~~
~~brought to my mind a vague suggestion of a country~~
~~as large as the United States. I do not know why,~~
~~but such was the case. I suppose it was because I~~
~~could not conceive of a small country having~~ so
large a history. ~~I think I was a little surprised to~~
~~find that the grand Sultan of Turkey was a man of~~
~~only ordinary size. I must try to reduce my ideas~~
~~of Palestine to a more reasonable shape. One gets~~
~~large impressions in boyhood, sometimes, which he~~
~~has to fight against all his life. "All these kings."~~
~~When I used to read that in Sunday school, it sug~~
~~gested to me the several kings of such countries as~~
~~England, France, Spain, Germany, Russia, etc. ar~~
~~rayed in splendid robes ablaze with jewels, march~~
~~ing in grave procession, with scepters of gold in their~~
~~hands and flashing crowns upon their heads. But~~

214

as the poems wrestle with each other. Some poems situate themselves as dialectical pivots, while others are pauses. For example, after the long sequence celebrating the Palestinian wedding of my sister, "A Concordance of Leaves," we pause at "Our Quiet Saturdays," a monologue sonnet from a Jewish Zionist perspective. I'd long been thinking about this man's perspective, one that I couldn't shake, compelling me to think of what it might be like to long to finally be in the majority in a country. When organizing a book, David Wojahn wisely notes that "the process comes down to an associative movement that lays special stress on the alternating need to both fulfill the reader's expectations regarding the book's movement but also to repeatedly confound them" (41). *Shrapnel Maps* foregrounds Palestinian loss, but in order to guide the reader to understand how that loss happened, and to try to imagine what a just peace might look like, I found it necessary, at times, to confound readerly expectations.

Second, *Shrapnel Maps* invites a reverse chronological reading, going backwards in time—even if that doesn't hold all the way through. I wanted to begin with seemingly universal poems that would invite every reader. But as the book proceeds, it digs further down to expose the conflict's deep roots, into global and local traumas—from colonialism to the Holocaust—that grip the land and its peoples. This reverse chronological structure suggests that, as Sue William Silverman recently shared, you cannot predict the past. Trauma is about revisitation. Necessarily, considering the past and its irruptions into the present requires a recursivity in poetic structure. As Susan Stewart writes, "There is not an instantaneous synthesis that results in poetic knowledge; rather, the forces of inspiration unfolding temporally in the form provide retrospective and recursive insight" (199). By the end of the book, readers have learned as well as experienced something more than an individual poem, or even series of poems, can usually contain.

Finally, the book is itself a kind of shrapneled map of (imagined) geographies of the land. We leap from place to place, Cleveland to Toura (West Bank), to Jerusalem/al-Quds, back to the US, to maps, to Jaffa, to Gaza, to exile and diaspora—all of these places and times reflecting different predicaments of subjectivity.

I want to say that the book grew like some sort of coral reef, beneath the surface of my consciousness, but that's not entirely true. It was more like building a house—you realize that, despite your floor plan, a necessary room is missing, and then another, and so on, until a shambling mansion grows where only an outbuilding once stood. I was scared by its size, but had a hard time imagining it any smaller. I felt such a weight—the weight of traumatic histories—that no book really could contain. I hope that I did some justice, or contributed to imagining another way, in the making of it. I hope that it hasn't added suffering to the ledger of existence. Its future is out of my hands.

The term "documentary poetics" seems too small a term, fixating on a formal procedure—working with documents—rather than on a poetic-political vision of reinventing the future by unearthing the past. The work of documentary/investigative poetry parallels the work of truth commissions—not only by gathering testimonies that haven't been aired widely, but also by examining, working with, and critiquing the political, legal, economic, and cultural systems that engineer oppression and injustice. Of course, a truth commission is a transitional justice mechanism for societies attempting to confront the past, reestablish the rule of law and governance, and move into the future. In the United States, perhaps we have arrived, at last, at a transitional justice moment—if there is political will to do this difficult yet transformational work. In the meantime, artists and activists have created a repository, a counterarchive, which provides a parallel cultural labor of undoing erasure, of making visible and audible a history that the official narratives suppress or exclude. It's critical to remember that archives began as ways of maintaining hegemony's memory through written records, so the counterarchive must see itself as something more fluid, more living, and less bound to documents—a laughing memory, a funeral dance, a mapped songline, worn prayer beads passed down. The counterarchive is not in a place, so a poetry book's relationship to that counterarchive will be like a thumbnail, jump drive, or hyperlink.

The work continues. Each time I embark on a new book, it's as if I've never done it before. I want to surprise myself with some new way of shaping a work, not repeat myself. As I'm trying to finish a new book about migration and belonging, I'm holding this advice as I try different combinations of the manuscript:

1. Start your manuscript with the strongest poem, end with the second strongest. A.E. Stallings writes, "put the strong poems first, and a strong closing poem." Do you have a poem that is a kind of skeleton key, an *ars poetica*, to the work?

    a.   *Counterpoint: A poem's strength is somewhat subjective, so you'll have to rely on your gut and what trusted readers tell you.*

2.   Keep only your strongest work. Kelli Russell Agodon writes: "'When in doubt, take it out.' A reader will not miss what they never read, but they will remember the clunker left in. Shorter manuscripts do better in contests." Most contemporary books of poems have about fifty to seventy-five pages of poetry, and ballast weighs down the ship of our book. You can always save some poems once the work is taken and ask if the publisher thinks they're necessary.

    a.   *Counterpoint: some essential recent books weigh in at around two hundred pages, like Tyehimba Jess's* Olio *or M. NourbeSe Philip's* Zong!

3.   Physically engage with your paper copies of your poems, trying out organizational strategies. Teresa Mei Chuc writes, "One of the best advice I ever got was to lay all of the pages on the floor and see how the poems interact with each other and which should go first and next." About that process, Naomi Shihab Nye writes, "Lay all the poems out on the floor of your study and let them befriend one another."

4.   Think of what draws your poems together. Michael Bazzett writes, "look at first lines and last lines, and try to have them hold hands, when possible." Simeon Berry believes poems in a book should be "like links in a chain, so that there's a rise and fall between each segment, but each segment locks together in a unit."

    a.   *Counterpoint: sometimes your poems do battle with each other as well (Blake: no progression without contraries).*

5.   Revise your poems with the other poems of the book in mind. Even good published poems might need some condensing.

6.   Create a working title that might speak to the book's contexture. How does the title help create a frame for the entire book?

7. Relatedly, find the structure and structuring metaphor that corresponds best to your burgeoning book. Is it a dwelling, like George Herbert's *The Temple*? Is it a journey, like Dante's *Divine Comedy*? Is it a mapping, like Elizabeth Bishop's *North and South*? For books that employ autobiographical narrative, pay attention to how they tell their story—if it's a temporal structure at all. Is it best to begin at the beginning? Somewhere *in medias res*? Or with a reverse chronology? Jennifer Sperry Steinorth writes "think about what information is revealed when—so that the poems enhance one another in terms of story, metaphor and other kinds of meaning making."

    a. *Counterpoint: Lauren Shapiro writes, "rather than strict chronology or distinct sections, I like to think of a manuscript as comprised of waves. This means I think about how poems work with the ones near them, and how these waves work together to make something larger."*

8. Consider braiding a series of crucial poems throughout the manuscript—what Nancy Reddy called a "scattered series." The "scattered series" may also be photographs, drawings, or ephemera that comprise a ghost archive, some wider repository toward which the poems gesture.

9. Use the paratextual elements of a manuscript—the table of contents, blank pages, section breaks, images—to offer breathing space for the reader, silences to leave unspoken, mysteries to explore further, and resting places before a pivoting.

10. Read your own book aloud, from cover to cover, to see how it sounds—and rely on friends to tell you when to hold on and keep working, and when to let it go into the world.

One final, large counterpoint from Erin Belieu:

> Many of my MFA/PhD students recently think their books must be "concept" books in order for any press to be interested in the work. I tried to explain that this is not the case. A "collection" of poems is called a collection for a reason. That is, if you have a genuine, driving artistic passion that turns out to be conceptual, great. Obviously some wonder-

ful and critically acclaimed books in recent years come to mind. But don't think you have to strain to cook up some pre-digested, overarching thematic for your book in order for it to have a strong point of view. Your particular consciousness *is* a point of view. I fear this impulse has to do with some pre-conceived idea of marketing and the prevalence of Lit theory classes more than the makerly instinct. (And I have a background in theory so am not one of those theory hating types at all.) I also privately polled three editor friends at major poetry presses to ask their opinion on this and all of them were like, "Ohmygod. EVERYTHING I'm seeing is written like this." One said, "I wish more emerging poets would just trust to their heart and soul in the poems they make."

Keep in mind that the fashion of today is the bellbottom of tomorrow; the technology of today is the eight-track of tomorrow. While it's impossible to read the tea leaves of our literary and human future, it's good to wonder: are you writing a book that someone would want to read next year? In ten years? After you've shaken off your breath for the last time?

Of course, a book is not the world. There is no total poem, no final poem, no matter what Rilke tells us about a poem containing the whole of life. But perhaps, as a poet, I have needed to believe it. Still, the work a poem—and a book of poems—can do may be smaller, but it is no less important—to hold a reader's attention, to reframe one person's window on the planet, creating a momentary refuge in the chaos and beautiful trouble of living.

Works Cited

Agodon, Kelli Russell. "Organizing a Book of Poems." *Facebook*. December 28, 2020. Time unknown. https://www.facebook.com/phil.metres/posts/10101090909490821. Accessed October 30, 2021.

Bazzett, Michael. "Organizing a Book of Poems." *Facebook*. December 28, 2020. Time unknown. https://www.facebook.com/phil.metres/posts/10101090909490821. Accessed October 30, 2021.

Belieu, Erin. "Organizing a Book of Poems." *Facebook*. December 28, 2020. Time unknown. https://www.facebook.com/phil.metres/posts/10101090909490821. Accessed October 30, 2021.

Berry, Simeon. "Organizing a Book of Poems." *Facebook*. December 28, 2020. Time unknown. https://www.facebook.com/phil.metres/posts/10101090909490821. Accessed October 30, 2021.

Chuc, Teresa Mei. "Organizing a Book of Poems." *Facebook*. December 28, 2020. Time unknown. https://www.facebook.com/phil.metres/posts/10101090909490821. Accessed October 30, 2021.

Friastat, Neil, ed. *Poems in Their Place: Intertextuality and Order of Poetic Collections*. UNC Press, 1987.

Huml, Gerald. "Assembling a Poetry Collection." Blog post. October 24, 2006. http://poetryexaminedlife.blogspot.com/2006/10/assembling-poetry-collection-below-are.html

Jameson, Fredric. *Postmodernism, or, the Cultural Logic of Late Capitalism*. Duke University Press, 1991.

Metres, Philip Metres. *Pictures at an Exhibition*. University of Akron Press, 2016.

——. *Sand Opera*. Alice James, 2015.

——. *Shrapnel Maps*. Copper Canyon, 2020.

——. *To See the Earth*. Cleveland State Poetry Center, 2008.

Nye, Naomi Shihab. "Organizing a Book of Poems." *Facebook*. December 28, 2020. Time unknown. https://www.facebook.com/phil.metres/posts/10101090909490821. Accessed October 30, 2021.

Reddy, Nancy. "Order Out of Chaos." *Poets & Writers*. Nov/Dec 2020. https://www.pw.org/content/order_out_of_chaos_revising_your_poetry_manuscript_0. Accessed October 30, 2021.

Ríos, Alberto. "Organization Strategies." http://ww.public.asu.edu/~aarios/resourcebank/02mssintofirstbook/page3.html. Accessed October 30, 2021.

Shapiro, Lauren. "Organizing a Book of Poems." *Facebook*. December 28, 2020. Time unknown. https://www.facebook.com/phil.metres/posts/10101090909490821. Accessed October 30, 2021.

Stallings, A. E. "Organizing a Book of Poems." *Facebook*. December 28, 2020. Time unknown. https://www.facebook.com/phil.metres/posts/10101090909490821. Accessed October 30, 2021.

Steinorth, Jennifer Sperry. "Organizing a Book of Poems." *Facebook*. December 28, 2020. Time unknown. https://www.facebook.com/phil.metres/posts/10101090909490821. Accessed October 30, 2021.

Stewart, Susan. *Poetry and the Fate of the Senses*. University of Chicago, 2002.

Wojahn, David. "'The Fiery Event of Every Day': Bishop, Reagan, and the Making of North & South." *The American Poetry Review*, vol 41, no. 6. 2012, pp. 39–45.

Dear Unexplainable

Kazim Ali

DEAR UNEXPLAINABLE,

How do you explain it?

During my undergraduate years at the University at Albany—where I imagined I would become a lobbyist, a lawyer, or a congressman, maybe in that order—I spent my days organizing rallies and phonebanks or collecting signatures on postcards to send to state legislators, and nights hanging out with my friends and that strange central structure called by the university the Podium. A "podium" in most cases being the lectern from which a professor lectured—still the most common pedagogy of those days—but at the University at Albany, mother of my wisdom, the word referred to that architectural feature of the campus that connected every academic building, an open air series of plazas and galleries around a large central pool and fountain, rumored at the time to have been based on the government complex in Tehran, Iran and intended to be built not for the University at Albany but the University of Arizona in Tucson. There was even a verb in our local parlance for hanging out on the Podium: we called it "podiating." Anyhow, the Podium probably would have been better a structure for the other university—that desert site with its holy wind—than the northern part of New York, huddled against the Hudson River, and given to frigid winters that would send blasts of wind roaring through its pillared galleries. Nonetheless, the milieu felt mythical: and provided many a venue for late night feverish arguments about poetry, philosophy, politics. My real degree was in wandering. My faculty was the night, the syllabi hand-rolled and smoked, the diploma only ashes. A poem is a kind of building too, and a book of poems a kind of Podium. You must find your own way to travel through it. The writer has an advantage—a book would naturally be opened at the beginning and read left-to-right (at least in English) to the end—but the reader can always dodge or upend the design: begin in the middle, consult the table of contents and choose a poem by title, riffle through, read the end first. The writer's advantage is strong, to be sure, but in the face of a rebellious reader there's no contest as to who wins.

I suppose assembling a book has the same architectural considerations as composing a poem. That might only be true if you think of a poem (as I do) as more of an "event," a confluence of various energies, a "text" (weave) to be experienced (through various sensory organs of the body, not solely the mind). I imagine a poet might conceive of a poem as a piece of writing (or music: that's Hugo's binary, "music" vs "meaning") in which one constructs in language an experience of the writer's for the reader to read/interpret. I've written poems in which that was my primary intention, but—

Maybe that's all I'll say about that in the beginning. When I first thought of publishing a book (is it a book of poems? or a book of poetry? "Poems" and "poetry" being not necessarily the same thing. Also, how do you feel about the terms "volume" or "collection?" These two also imply different organizing principles) I mostly thought in terms of a sustained project. This was from my primary literary practices at the time: I'd been reading small (sixty to a hundred pages) books of prose (essay, fiction, uncategorizable) and they inspired me (*House of Incest* by Anaïs Nin, *Thomas the Obscure* by Maurice Blanchot, *generations* by Lucille Clifton) in the direction of the cohesion of theme that is possible in an extended (but not *too extended*) exploration.

Helen Elam first taught Blanchot's criticism to me; and then handed me Blanchot's odd, elusive fiction as well when I took to him. The novel I loved best had been translated by Pierre Joris, another of the faculty members at the University. Elam was the professor who taught the seminar on literary criticism I took as part of my major requirements, and she was mostly interested in post-structuralist thought. I learned post-structuralism and deconstruction before I learned any other kind of criticism. To this day, I am skeptical when someone—*anyone*—says "you have to learn the rules before you break them." Whose rules? What if the way I think (or read or write) is because it's the way I think and not meant as a "breaking" of whatever rule *you* have about poetry or fiction or writing itself? I learned the beauty of the break before ever knowing what it was that had been broken. That's how life is for some of us.

As far as assembling a book of poems goes, I developed an affection for the serial approach (in many of Susan Howe's books from 1989 onward, but particularly apparent in *The Nonconformist's Memorial* and *Pierce-Arrow*) as well as the book that interrogated a theme, whether or not it used precisely the same formal approach throughout (*The End of Beauty* and *Swarm* by Jorie Graham, Michael Palmer's books *First Figure*, *Sun*, and *Notes from Echo Lake*, Donald Revell's books *There Are Three* and *Arcady*). The "collection" itself assembled, resonated, circled back on itself, made echoes of its own sounds. My metaphors are from music because I happen to agree with Hugo: he thought that truth ought to conform to music, and that poetry in which music conformed to truth was inferior work.

When I stayed in the master's program to study critical theory, I forged a path yet unknown in academic circles: I continued studying theory with Helen Elam, but rather than specialize, I simultaneously studied translation with Pierre Joris, poetry with Judith Johnson, and even took a dive into Cultural Studies, taking a class with the brilliant and fearsome Marxist critic Teresa Ebert, who gave me a dreaded B-minus on my final paper, writing dramatically across the last page a single damning comment: "Ludic." I stuck with her for another class, determined to learn what she had to teach. For my master's thesis, a long time before one could do such a thing without raising eyebrows, I wrote a novel and an accompanying critical paper. It's common enough in hybrid programs these days, but I assure you it was unheard of in 1995, at least in the circles I was running in.

When—after a stint in lobbying, organizing, and nonprofit administration—I went back to graduate school for creative writing, I shed my skin and changed my spots in between my first and second years, and came back to workshop with a whole different kind of poem. Gone were the plaintive lyrics (informed no doubt by the Farsi and Urdu poetry I'd listened to throughout my life) and prayerful divinations (likely the same provenance), and a new, more disjunctive poem appeared, the surface more distressed (in both emotive and painterly senses), the cores more unstable (geologically and semiotically). It alarmed both fellow students and faculty.

I'd gone to France to visit family that summer and while there I left the safe confines of Paris (where my uncle, aunt, and cousins lived) and wandered the south for a month, purposely because I couldn't speak French. I wanted to be (in that impossible yearning of the young earnest poet) without language. It worked and it didn't. Worked because I wrote voluminous pages of fractured little lyrics, an artistic practice that has haunted my writing ever since. At the time it was because I was living in a language I could only understand bits and scraps of. As I navigated my daily life trying to express myself, I would stutter or hop from expression to expression, helped along by whomever I might be talking to. Fluency was not an option. And so my mode of expression in language while speaking necessarily came to impact what and how I wrote. Didn't work because, true to form, my ear wouldn't relent and by the end of the month of wandering alone through Marseille, Cassis, and across the island of Corsica and back, I'd more or less learned traveling French. Bar French. Café French. But the stilted, broken syntax continued to linger in the poems I wrote. Somehow amid the shards I found great resonance, the potential for a meaning beyond what fluency might circumscribe. To be "fluent" is to "know," and to me the province of poetry was the beyond, the unknown, the startling, the misunderstood.

In the influent, the cacophonous, one finds in such poems other qualities of music: the reverb, the echo, the grace notes, the concord and discord, the quirky minor key, cadences and fadeouts, and most exciting to me, overtones and undertones. A poem of scattered approach actually holds infinite meaning inside, portals and paths in a dozen or a hundred directions. And who is the person who is writing such a coruscating encounter of text? As Deleuze and Guattari wrote of their collaborative writing—thank you Helen Elam for putting such books in a poet's hands—"Since each of us was several, there was already quite a crowd" (1).

It was these radioactive pages from Provence and Corsica that I came back with and intended to turn into a thesis, though after I came back to New York I did not rediscover my ability to write in whole sentences and lines. Fracture came with me. Or perhaps it's better to say that it was released. The seriality I spoke of earlier enabled a forward motion. Like a painter who created canvas after canvas in order to explore the limits of a concept or medium, I wrote and wrote, in order to interrogate the method itself. After reading sixty pages of short five to eight-line lyrics, all fractured, as if they were a collection of Sapphic scraps, my thesis advisor, Mark Doty, nudged me in a different direction. "When I read a book," he said, "I like the ones that read like record albums." He was talking about the vinyl 12" discs which were once (along with the newer-fangled 8-track and eventually smaller 16-track cassettes) the primary mode of a musician releasing their music. A twelve-inch vinyl only had so much space on it. Most pop musicians could fit five songs to a side. If a song was longer there might only be four. It was a controlled environment and with only so much space. The notion of a dynamic shift of forms between poems appealed to me. Mark loaned me a copy of Ronald Johnson's (then out-of-print and not much discussed) epic book *ARK*. I was intrigued by the way Johnson built momentum with various forms and shapes throughout the book. As far as individual poems go, Mark suggested I read Barbara Guest. I discovered Guest's *Rocks on a Platter*, her own ars poetica on "arrangement," both of a book and a poem itself. In her reckoning there was something very physically sculptural and gestural about arranging the parts of a poem—a line describing a physical phenomenon would lie next to an abstraction, which would be followed by a line of dialogue. Berrigan's beautiful *Sonnets* too opened this mode for me. I was surprised to find the same advice from Doty, Guest, and Berrigan.

In that way, my MFA thesis manuscript was a musical sampler of various types of poems I had been writing throughout my time in school. Dance tune followed by ballad. 4/4 rock beat followed by something Arab-inflected. Karma karma karma karma karma chameleon. You won't find a copy of it in the thesis library at NYU: on one of my invited readings back I snuck into the library at the Lillian Vernon House and stole it. It's in a box somewhere at my house. I imagine I'll give it back someday. We'll see. My little six-lined bits alternated with long-lined chants and rants, prose poems, and even some graphic poems inspired by the city's life itself. In other words, the music of that first manuscript was a music of disruption and multiple perspectives. It would be a few years still before I listened to Alice Coltrane's album *Universal Consciousness* and came to understand that even in what sounds like "disruption" or "disjunction," individual consciousness could coalesce. That there *was* a relationship between what we as humans in minds and bodies think of as "chaos" or "unity." There is a swirl in the world. One fashions a journey as a sculptor might or a choreographer. I left the city soon after for work. I couldn't find any in the city that would sustain me, and I was offered a position teaching first-year writing at The Culinary Institute of America up the Hudson River. I lived in Rhinebeck, at that time a sort of sleepy river town in northern Dutchess County and began a rigorous yoga practice. In the days after the buildings fell and the war(s) started I began to dance with a local company. Gesture in breath and body (through yoga and dance) defined my daily life, and coupled with the food that my students were cooking every day, my life shifted on its axis a little bit from being a life of the mind and mouth to being a life of the body and still: the mouth.

For several years after that I tried to publish my two books—the original thematically and formally unified thesis and the second wildly diverse iteration. All the while I was writing new poems. Eventually I had more new poems than old. When I hit a hundred and one pages (that odd number significant in my numerologically obsessed culture: think the 1,001 nights, a slight mistranslation of the Arabic, which would more literally be rendered "One thousand nights and one night"), I chose two fellow poets to send them to. One was Jennifer Chapis, a poet with whom I had never been in a workshop, but nonetheless developed a close relationship with—we would go on to found Nightboat Books together the following year—and Kathleen Graber, a friend who was in a couple of workshops with me. There was another important difference: Jennifer and I shared a lot of aesthetic views, while Kathy and I constantly (and good-naturedly) argued on opposite sides of most questions while in workshop. I wanted divergent views and only two.

As I suspected, Jennifer and Kathy chose different selections. Jennifer chose fifty pages, the fifty pages I liked the most, but was unsure of. Kathy chose only thirty-two pages, but with a kind warning that she didn't think she was the right reader for me, and I shouldn't take her thoughts too seriously. Of the two selections, only eighteen poems overlapped. I started with Kathy's thirty-two as the core of the book. The reader always has it over on the writer, as I've said. The first trick might be the writer's—the form of the book—but it's a trick of pure accident. It depends on compliance. The *real* creator of the form of the book of the poetry *is* the reader because she (Kathy in this case) is the one who creates it. There was an element of trust, or as Louise Glück has said about the relationship between a teacher and a student, the sole power one has is to choose the instrument by which one is changed (108).

The poetry books I loved the most were on the shorter side. Mine was about seventy-five pages. Several more years passed while I tried to publish it. It was a semi-finalist, then a finalist, at several contests. Again and again and again. Eventually in the spring of 2004, I put it aside and began to work on new poems. That August I had to go to California for a month. I was taking the young student chefs and restauranteurs from The Culinary Institute of America, on a month-long seminar to study food and drink, learning about terroir and fabrication of various kinds. I printed out a copy of the manuscript to take with me. For that month, traveling between the farms of the Central Valley, the vineyards of Sonoma and Napa, and the restaurants of San Francisco (as well as factories—Torani syrup, Jelly Belly, Scharffen Berger chocolate, St. George's Distilleries—we ate and drank well), I worked on the poems, handwriting revisions, crossing out lines, writing new poems in the margins, reordering pages. When I came home, I felt I had a real start on the book. That the manuscript could be a book. There was a wrinkle: try as I might, I could not find the manuscript—or any of the drafts of the manuscript—in my laptop files. I cannot explain what happened, but the only version of the poems I had left was the printout scrawled with corrections. I had to type the manuscript anew from scratch. The process of re-typing, reconfiguring, meant each line, each poem was new: I couldn't just type "corrections" in. The order, the new poems, the poems I yanked. Somehow, the book shrank from seventy-five pages to around fifty pages. Long poems were condensed: one three-and-a-half-page meander ended up as the ten-line poem "Renunciation," which opens the collection. Jane Cooper was a titular spirit here in terms of the book as a whole with its political commitments, its dedication to allowing silences to speak, and Niedecker guided me as far as individual poems went. I condensed and condensed. That was the book that became *The Far Mosque*.

There's a story that gets told about a poet's second books: that they're worse. That you spend your entire life up until a point doing your first book, and if it happens to be successful, your second book comes fast—*too* fast. Fifteen years to write a first book, three to write a second? Some poets do take their time between books. Ilya Kaminsky published books fifteen years apart. Twenty-six years passed between Eleanor Lerman's second and third books. In Kaminsky's case he was writing, editing, and translating the whole time; Lerman, after devastating reviews and the pressures of the literary world, withdrew from writing and was only coaxed back by Sarah Gorham, who would eventually publish Lerman's comeback volume and a couple more after that, besides. As it happened, I (mostly) wrote my second book in an afternoon. It was in that in-between stage when I had put the manuscript of *The Far Mosque* aside. It was a July afternoon in the Hudson Valley. I was languorous. I had been reading Meena Alexander's collection *Illiterate Heart* and something about the form of the short lyric, always fractured at its close, resonated. I had loose-leaf paper, the kind with holes punched through for a school binder. I began writing poems. I wrote thirty-two drafts in one afternoon. I did twelve more in the week that followed. The exercise was the start of my fifteen-year long friendship with Alexander. I reached out to her by email to tell her what happened; she approved of the concept of writing a book *as* a book and invited me down to New York for tea.

I worked on the book as a book for several more years after that. Though I revised and edited extensively and though some pieces didn't make it all the way through the editing process, I didn't add too many new poems. *The Fortieth Day* is mostly comprised of poems whose original drafts I wrote that afternoon. This alternation between the quick and the prolonged continued throughout all the books I wrote that followed. *Sky Ward* was the compilation of almost seven years of work, but I wrote *Bright Felon* in three quick months; *Inquisition* collected work of nearly ten years—reaching back into my notebooks and including poems I had written as early as graduate school—then I wrote *The Voice of Sheila Chandra* in a single calendar year, most of that in three individual months (May, September, and November). The book I am working on now is comprised of individual pieces I worked on over the space about five or six years, but a few of the poems I am most excited about are written from drafts nearly twenty years old, drafts I'd long abandoned. Such a book is an arrangement in time, a sediment, a history and an event all at once, but all events in history are like that: manifestations of a chain of causal events, both known and unknown, historical, political, social, familial, that may stretch back many thousands of years.

After all, a poet is a wanderer ultimately, maybe even a wanderer in the pages of their own book. A wanderer in a maze or labyrinth cannot be expected to find their way straight out, but rather the wandering itself becomes the journey. One may wander in the labyrinth and end their days. In *The Fortieth Day*, there are poems called "Morning Prayer," "Afternoon Prayer," "Evening Prayer," and "Night Prayer," scattered throughout the manuscript. Lest you think I structured it too much, I'll share that there are five daily prayers in Islam (whose philosophy governs that book); one prayer is missing. There are repeated phrases and words in poems with quite different forms. I have poems named after the seasons and months ("The Year of Winter," "The Year of Summer," "The Year of Autumn," and so on, "December," "July," "September," and so on) scattered through my books. Some stations are unstaffed, subjects for future poems.

Sky Ward has the story of Icarus built through it, but it's not complete: Icarus is left at a tenuous, cliff-hanging moment, though not the one you might remember from the myth; *Bright Felon* works backward in time taking for its chapter titles the cities I have lived in, though one city is missing. In a book, something should always be missing. The twin brothers Hesperus and Phosphorus haunt the three long poems of *The Voice of Sheila Chandra*, though the astute historian of astronomy will know that that the heavenly bodies thought by the Greeks to be twins were one body all along, the planet Venus. I always reach back and reach forward. Icarus climbed out of the ocean after all. He grew. He survived a trauma in which a thousand generations of listeners and readers imagined he perished. He lived. He turned fifty.

I always think in a book there should be a secret, something that isn't shared, either with the poems or with the reader, something the poet is doing, some energy or technique or theme or even word that lies within the work unknown yet animating it, the way unknown moons or planets may pull with distant gravities bodies (of humans and of water) on the Earth. This could be an image, a phrase, an approach in the poem, something Barbara Guest called "the invisible architecture" of the poem and the book. *Rocks on a Platter* enacted the ways different parts of a book or poem could resonate against one another. In any event, I'm less interested in poetry (or music or dance or painting) that feels "finished" (read: "concluded") and more interested in art (and writing) that spills beyond the frame or page or stage. Music lingers in the ear. A book should be alive. When we wandered the Podium, arguing, reciting poetry to each, sometimes lying entwined in the gardens and courtyards—when I later wandered the Earth from Palestine to Patagonia, from the Himalayan foothills to the Continental Divide—I learned that the dance, like the poem, like the book, is a place where things happen. There are always three—the poet, the poem, and the reader. In every way, a poem is a place I try to remember what my language is, where my home is, how it is I can live. I don't know if a reader will ever find a place there. And yet I offer that space. I create in hopes of such a response. Publishing a poem is a small gamble; publishing a book feels like full-blown terror. Why do it at all? Because the reader has to complete the last part of the creative process. It is not written until it is given and received.

The Podium we see is only one part of it. Because of those frigid gusts constantly blowing during Albany's winter months, it's nearly impossible to walk between buildings on the surface. But luckily enough there are subterranean tunnels from building to another. When I was at school it was even rumored that there were more tunnels than we knew about, secret tunnels leading from the Podium to the residential quads and to various outer buildings. My friends and I made a game of it: we looked and looked, but we never found them.

Works Cited

Deleuze, Gilles and Felix Guattari. *A Thousand Plateaus: Capitalism and Schizophrenia*, translated by Brian Massumi. University of Minnesota Press, 1987.

Glück, Louise. *Proofs and Theories: Essays on Poetry*. Ecco Press, 1994.

Guest, Barbara. "Invisible Architecture," *Forces of Imagination: Writing on Writing*. Kelsey Street Press, 2002, pg. 18.

Guest, Barbara. *Rocks on a Platter: Notes on Literature*. Wesleyan University Press, 1999.

Hugo, Richard. *The Triggering Town: Lectures and Essays on Poetry and Writing*. W. W. Norton, 2010.

Mystery and Legacy in Shaping a Manuscript

Cyrus Cassells

AS MY HERO-POET Federico García Lorca once said, "only mystery allows us to live, only mystery" (1). I'd augment Lorca's dictum: "only mystery allows us to live and to write and to grow." Vis-à-vis composition and growth, I find my poetry is consistently two years ahead of my day-to-day self, so I've learned to pay attention, sometimes like a fogbound Sherlock Holmes, to its lures and messages. Whatever my work might signify to the public or my readers, for my part, my verse is a relentless and tireless mirror, an indispensable tool for self-awareness and bona fide revelation. Usually, by the time a volume is published, I have a much firmer grasp of the why of the book and the place the poems occupy in the meaningful arc of my entire life. The gist of the poetry effectively points me toward my deepest obsessions, fears, strivings, and my most authentic self—a self free of others' projections and judgments; I've discovered that the poems are often invariably wiser than the everyday or historical Cyrus.

I'm an unusual poet in that I work almost exclusively in book-length cycles; it often takes several years for the full "theme" of the cycle to emerge, which can be both frustrating and exhilarating in terms of the dogged detective work and ever-expanding odyssey required. In my forty-year career, I've hardly ever written an occasional poem. I seem to crave length and structure as a poet; my lyric impulses are almost always linked to a far-ranging project. I'm a world citizen and inveterate traveler, so crafting my thematic books often involves actual pilgrimage, cultural investigation, and historical study. I am consistently drawn to the past, to places of trauma (Hiroshima, Auschwitz, Dresden), and to stories of hard-won spiritual triumph.

I am also a professional actor, and my written work has something of a mediumistic quality; I seldom write from the perspective of Cyrus, and often take on the personae of other people—ideally performing this artistic "channeling" without appropriation or exploitation but with true identification and inmost respect. The chameleon impulse is very much how I live; I readily whisk past the usual social and physical boundaries to explore the psychologies and predicaments of my poetic speakers: my life and poetry are centered in an active and purposeful notion of identification and communion. The gauge for me in crafting a persona poem is the veracity of the presented voice and a willingness to do justice in conveying another human experience. This requires as much diligent research, integrity, and fluent empathy as I can muster in service to the poem—just as I would study for a demanding acting role, such as Shakespeare's tragic general Othello, which I have played on more than one occasion. I have also been in the poignant and challenging position of having people request and petition me to tell their stories (this was particularly the case in crafting my war-related volumes, *Soul Make a Path through Shouting* and *The Crossed-Out Swastika*) with the aim of documenting what they themselves have been unable to express in language.

I'd like to focus on the process of my third book, *Beautiful Signor*, though the journey with this project was far less mysterious than the process with my other books. Though this volume is the one most rooted in my personal and everyday life, there were, nevertheless, surprises and revelations waiting for me. Because a discerning reader of my previous books had questioned me as to why I never seemed to write about Cyrus, I set myself the task with *Beautiful Signor* of using the elating ingredients of a given day or encounter in my new life as an Italian language student and professional actor living in Florence and Rome: hence, the abundance of place-oriented titles, such as "Love Poem with the Cacophony of Rome" and "Love Poem with the Ruins of Ostia." The result, in terms of structure, was several strings of ecstatic, episodic lyrics, placed like poetic garlands or iridescent necklaces throughout *Beautiful Signor*. I ordered the lyrics, rooted in my brand-new life as an expatriate, to create a mini-documentary about my overseas romances and adventures, based on motif, key imagery, and location (the book makes side trips to France, Greece, Malta, and Tunisia, but is set primarily set in Italy). One of the surprises is that even though *Beautiful Signor* is based on my actual life experiences, the I of the poems still remains, for my part, a verse creation, akin to a theatrical mask or a romantic persona: a self-made myth.

Beautiful Signor was always meant to be upbeat and celebratory—as a way to defuse some of the adversarial debate about gay intimacy and love. My goal with *Beautiful Signor* was to create an ebullient gay text that was a hundred-percent tenderness: "Your cupped hands / I drink from, regal, insistent, / your cradling, penny-colored eyes, / persuade me / wherever there's a lover's solicitous gaze, / unscripted joy, / the Nazarene still walks the wounded earth, / in unwavering tenderness..." (Cassells 2). My plan was to go forth in the spirit of the *Song of Songs* and Nobel Laureate Juan Ramón Jiménez's beloved text about a boy's boundless love for his donkey, *Platero and I*.

The impulse to create *Beautiful Signor* arose, typical of me, out of outrage and politics. I wrote it during the period of Senator Jesse Helms's ravings, amid a battery of poisonous public discourse about gay art and people. I wanted to share what I'd experienced of male love beyond the mainstream's hostile notions of gay sexuality. Certainly the two urges toward joy and outcry, defiant love and protest, are not necessarily opposed, which is why, at moments, the specter of homophobia and of the AIDS crisis appear as keen shadows in the praise songs, as in "Love Poem with the Wind of Calvary": "I am not disease only; / hold me as you would hold / the body of Christ" (Cassells 3).

I lost four of my friends to AIDS in 1992—the year I went to Italy and began *Beautiful Signor*—and I think, for my own sanity and equilibrium, I wanted to focus not only on mourning and the long ghastly arm of the AIDS crisis but also on the brave eureka of gay connection; I wanted to fashion a honeymoon book for gay people, and to make it, in addition, a homoerotic garden in which anyone could stroll and feel comfortable, feel communion. In *Beautiful Signor*, I placed gay content beside traditional (that is, heteronormative romantic tropes): castles and moats, doves, Pegasus, grottoes, balconies, magical forests, manna, the hideaway for lovemaking—all very traditional Western tropes. My strategy was deliberate: the book's aim became to use time-tested tropes and wed them to a celebration of bonding, "the wild sweet work of union," as I call it in my Crete-set poem "Arc" (Cassells 4). I wanted to underline "we have our moons and Junes and flowers and guitars and all of that, too—if we're only willing to claim them!" Ultimately, I viewed this poetic project as recovery work, a healing process that involved legitimizing gay rapture and romance in familiar Western romantic terms.

Another mission was to create erotic poetry that suited my individual temperament. It's both easy and commonplace to write badly about sex—to go into a kind of delirious soft focus—that shuts out specificity and authenticity, the way saxophones and candles seem to cue in generic sexiness in facile, derivative movies and TV. It's lazy shorthand. Beauty and inventiveness save sexual descriptions from triteness. As a poet, I'm drawn to sonic beauty and indirection in erotic writing; I think it allows readers a way "into" sexual experience that in-your-face, purplish, or generic writing doesn't permit. I loved the description of the dancing desert boy in *The English Patient*: "the pure beauty of an innocent dancing boy, like sound from a boy chorister, which he remembered as the purest of sounds, the clearest river water, the most transparent depths of the sea. Here in the desert, which had been an old sea, where nothing was strapped down or permanent, everything drifted—like the shift of linen across the boy as if he were embracing or freeing himself from an ocean or his own blue afterbirth" (Ondaatje 5). I found Michael Ondaatje's subtleties in his widely lauded novel incredibly haunting and transcendently erotic. At first glance, some of the descriptive passages in *Beautiful Signor* might seem like euphemism or double entendre but at the core, my work in my third book was about making romantic and erotic moments entrancing and beautiful on the page, in the mouth.

Often I was working with the troubadour trope, as in my opening poem, "Guitar": "We're troubadours / because we've learned, / from the burrs of plague and war: / life on earth is / brief, keen incendiary" and in "Love Poem of the Pyrenees": "sex is a troubadour's pulse / a song: // bivouac of twilight / bridge of mountain dawn" (Cassells 6; 7). *Beautiful Signor*'s original title was *The Troubadours Are Still in Rome*. On finishing the book, I found one of the revealed mysteries was that my project blossomed to embrace not only gay love but also the metaphysical concept of The Beloved, of finding God, the logos, in the gaze and body of one's lover ("all this majesty is for me," as I say in the poem "The Hummingbird")—a concept more fully fleshed out in Sufi poetry and culture than in traditional Western culture (Cassells 8). The troubadour became the dervish, The Beloved became the *Beautiful Signor* of the title, a phrase which I borrowed from gay poet Aaron Shurin. The Beautiful Signor of the title is both a real person and an exemplar of the spirit of romantic love: "What the Sufis, the headlong / troubadours acclaimed, / the dervishes danced toward— / the worthy risk, / the wild-hearted gift, / scintilla of heaven— / you are, you are, / Beautiful Signor" (Cassells 9).

In the tradition of the *Song of Songs* and Saint John of the Cross, the poems of *Beautiful Signor* reiterate the longing to experience romantic, erotic love as a gateway to spiritual realization. I created a poem, "Amalgam," about an impromptu gay wedding, as an enhancing coda: "But look, as ever, / we spat-upon lovers live, / pledged men. // In you, the foothold, / the firmament. // In you, in you, / altar bread, justice, / the attar of home" (Cassells 10). Then I found a quote from Yeats that seemed to put a ribbon on my journey with this book, an upbeat project determined to celebrate gay unions in the face of hatred and incomprehension: "All dreams of the soul end in a beautiful man's or woman's body." Another surprise: two decades after the book was composed, I ended up experiencing an impromptu same-sex wedding ceremony in a sacred space, just as in "Amalgam" (Cassells 11). I consider this coincidence as one example of how a poem has served as portent or prophesy in my life.

The notion of a honeymoon book for gay people kept me determined to sustain the note of wedding-bed ecstasy and intimacy, the adoring gaze, from start to finish. For me personally, when I reread *Beautiful Signor*, which is the longest of all of my nine volumes so far, the emphasis on lovemaking and pleasure, the aura of prolonged rapture is its most impres-

sive feature: the jubilant tone never flags or becomes pedestrian, reminding me that dynamic literature doesn't necessarily have to arise from rue,
discontent, or restlessness. *Beautiful Signor* has had the widest and most
diverse range of fans of my all work, including a monk in a Michigan abbey
who set some of the key poems to classical music and gifted me with the
score. The fact that the book has appealed to both gay and straight readers
has been profoundly gratifying, especially since one of my goals was to
create a blissful homoerotic garden that anyone could visit and relish as
co-dreamers and co-adventurers.

I don't believe in formulas for writing, so I hope my discussion of the
making of my third book (published in 1997) will stand as a testament to
my belief in not-knowing, in patience, revision, time, and gradual revelation
as essential to shaping a vibrant and coherent manuscript. Besides intrepid
cutting (for instance, my ratio is usually 3 to 1 in terms of the final version
of a book), revision also means considering feedback by close readers or
allies that you can trust; reading your poems out loud to enhance aural
fluency as well as ease and poise on the page; and being open to new, surprising combinations and sequencing of your poems via playful experimentation: I have sometimes placed all of my poems on the floor and picked
them up at random to consider newer and maybe wilder juxtapositions.

In regard to legacy, each poem is a record of the breath and body of
the poet, and each book represents one's artistic and spiritual journey and
patrimony. With the exception of one book cover, I have chosen the art
for all of my other seven books, so when I look at the titles on my bookshelf
there is a visual and aesthetic continuity that pleases me and faithfully
represents my aesthetics—a visual as well as a poetic signature.

Turkish Nobel Laureate Orhan Pamuk declares in his masterly novel,
My Name is Red: "The beauty and mystery of this world only emerge
through affection, attention, interest and compassion…open your eyes
wide and actually see this world by attending to its colors, details, and
irony" (Parmuk 12). My final advice in shaping a poetry manuscript, in
considering its truest pattern and essence, is to become all-patient, even
well-acquainted and at ease with mystery and, as Albert Einstein once
advised, to "never lose a holy curiosity" (13).

Works Cited

Cassells, Cyrus. *Beautiful Signor*. Copper Canyon Press, 1997.

Einstein, Albert: "Old Man's Advice to Youth: Never Lose a Holy Curiosity." *Life* Magazine: May 2, 1955.

Lorca, Federico García, *The Book of the Drawings of Federico García Lorca*. Tabapress/Fundación Federico García Lorca, 1990.

Ondaatje, Michael. *The English Patient*. Knopf, 1992.

Parmuk, Orhan. *My Name is Red,* translated by Erdağ M. Göknar. Knopf, 2001.

Yeats, William Butler. *The Wild Swans at Coole*. Cuala Press, 1917.

Of Bonsais and Moons

An Epistolary on Making a Book of Poems

Victoria Chang

DEAR POET,

At some point, you may decide that you would like to do more than write poems, that you might want to assemble an entire collection of your poems. Maybe you decided this even before you began writing your first poem, or after you had written six poems or six hundred poems. Maybe you decided this after you had read a book of poems that gave you the sensation of falling. Or rising.

Assembling, writing, or wrangling a book of poems is a lot like writing a single poem. The book itself is a poem (I read that Robert Frost said something similar—that the book itself is the *final poem*), though no one can seem to find this quote, which is appropriate because no one really knows where a poem comes from either, let alone a book of poems.

I secretly think all poems come from the moon. I would have thought most of my poems were inscriptions of the blood moon. But most of my poems are transpositions of the pink moon (the first full moon in April) and the more diplomatic flower moon (the first full moon in May).

There's also no one way of making a poem or book of poems. Just as a poem could be revised a thousand different ways, a book can be put together in a thousand and one different ways. Perhaps going into this process with this one thought—that there is no *one* way, can be freeing.

By the time you are ready to make your poetry book, you might have a stack of moons that glow a little on their own. You might feel that putting them together will be simple, compared to writing the poems. But you may soon discover that this is not true.

A book of poems is made of many different kinds of moons that may resist clarity and collectivism. But the book's goal is to *mark out a larger universe than the poems themselves do*, says poet G. C. Waldrep in an email exchange. Thus putting together a book of poems is the biggest and hardest poem you will write. And putting a book of poems together doesn't come from the moon. The moon has no interest in assembling. The moon is only interested in semblances. Making a book of poems comes entirely from you, the poet.

• • •

Lately I have been thinking about how the act of making a book of poems is similar to caring for bonsai plants. In my mother's last years, I inherited around fifty bonsais. These were not just any bonsais. These were the type that you'd find in the bonsai garden at the Huntington Library or the type in a courtyard on the other side of the world in the thirteenth century, under a blood moon.

Shortly before my mother died, I had started secretly giving the bonsai away one by one to anyone who would take them. When we had to move her to a facility, I picked ten and placed them on the small balcony, carrying them up the stairs, one by one, dropping them randomly on the balcony that overlooked a dilapidated apartment complex.

During the week of my mother's death, I managed to slide her into a wheelchair and roll her out to the balcony to look at her beloved bonsai. But she didn't care about them. She looked past them. To the moon. Which was already bright at noon.

These were bonsai that she had trimmed, pruned, watered, fertilized, and repotted for a decade before her death. She and my father had even made a small freeway of mini sprinklers that traveled to each, as well as a multilevel display that spanned a hundred feet, made out of cinder blocks and wooden shelving.

When my mother died, I gave away the remaining bonsai. I kept four, selected randomly. I sometimes wonder where those other bonsai are. If they are still alive. If they miss my mother. If they forgive me.

I kept those four bonsai alive for five years. Untrimmed, unloved, barely watered, alone. Then this year, one of my busier years, two unexpectedly died. One had the most beautiful wide and bulbous trunk. I could blame my job for this. I could blame the sun. I could blame the moon.

But I blame myself. I could have kept them alive but I didn't. As the five-year anniversary of my mother's death neared, I set out to keep the remaining two alive. I purchased special tools to care for them. I ordered hand-mixed soil. I learned how to care for them. One of the two is almost dead. While learning how to care for the remaining bits of my mother, I realized that caring for bonsai is similar to making a poetry book.

● ● ●

How, you might ask, especially if you've never taken care of a bonsai before? Imagine that you have inherited one. It is unruly. It is somewhat unrecognizable to you. You may have seen it or some of it somewhere before, at the corner of your eye, perhaps on your dead mother's display, somewhere in the middle on the top shelf, privately glistening amongst all the other plants.

You only slightly recognize it because a different you may have seen it once before, a you when your mother was alive. Similarly, your poems are from another you, from a moon that no longer exists. Each moon dies by morning. Each moon is the only one of its kind. The morning is elegy for that moon. Even so, each night, you still recognize the moon as a moon, despite never having met that particular moon before. This liminal space where the familiar and unfamiliar overlap is the space in which you will make a book of poems.

When you first adopt a bonsai, you will have to do some research on how other bonsais look. You might learn that there are *slanting trees, twin trunks, forests, windswepts, literatis, bonsai in rocks, root-over-rocks, formal uprights*, and more. You might also learn that you can make a bonsai out of almost any type of tree.

Similarly, you might open every poetry book you have on your shelf and look at their table of contents, flip through the books, not reading the poems, but thinking about their shapes, holding their girth in your hand. You might discover books with three sections, books with no sections, books with twelve sections, books composed entirely of one poem in the same form, books composed of poems in multiple forms, books composed entirely of individual poems.

If I select a few random books from my shelf, I see that *Ghost Of* by Diana Khoi Nguyen is in three sections with a frontispiece poem on its own; *The Gilded Auction Block* by Shane McCrae has four sections with one frontispiece poem (and there are illustrations within each section); *Stag's Leap* by Sharon Olds is divided by seasons but the poems mostly look the same in form; *The Tether* by Carl Phillips is also coincidentally divided into seasons but only two sections (August–December and January–May) where the poems vary in stanza lengths and use a lot of em dashes; *Sky Burial* by Dana Levin has no sections and many different types of poems, and *tea* by D. A. Powell is a landscape-shaped book divided into five sections labeled with titles such as *Tea Leaves*, *Tea Dance*, *Spilling Tea*, *Tea Rooms*, and *Reading Tea*, with poems that span the page horizontally and with rampant caesuras.

While researching, something to observe is your own development as a writer. If you're writing a first book, is it helpful to look at the twelfth book of a poet? Maybe, but you might want to remember to organize your notes by first book, second book, third book, etc.; otherwise, you might read a poet's twelfth book and become discouraged. That poet might have a lot more experience than you, and a twelfth book is likely different than a first book.

If you've spent an hour looking through your bookshelves, you'll discover that there's nothing more pleasurable than looking at a book of poems without actually having to do the hard work of reading the poems. There's nothing that needs to be done at this stage but to receive the brilliance and ideas of others before you. Part of being a poet is acknowledging that you are a descendant first, poet second.

• • •

If you inherited a bonsai, you might put it on a table and sit in front of it for a while and just look at it. You might not judge it or ask anything of it, you might just receive it. At some point, after you've looked long enough, you might start asking the bonsai questions such as, *who are you, what shape do you want to be, what are you proudest of, do you like your trunk, what are the shape of your leaves, what bonsais do you admire and why...?*

In the same way, you might look at your poems for a while without any judgment. Some people like to lay them on the floor or on a long table—I prefer the floor because I have no table that long or that clean. The *without any judgment* part is probably the hardest part. Do you judge the moon? You probably accept the new moon each night. Sometimes you might admire its size. Other times, you might marvel at its violence. Can you do the same thing with your own progeny of the moon?

Once you have looked and really seen your poems in a new way, you can then take an inquiry-based approach to learn more about them. Ask them questions out loud. Hear your own voice ask the questions and listen to the words (if there are any) that return. Your poems may just return a color or send wind past your ear. Whatever it says, listen carefully. Whatever it doesn't say, listen carefully to the silence.

Some questions you might ask are:

- How are you today?
- What kind of mood are you in? Does your mood ever change?
- Are you a nice set of poems, angry, curious, playful? Are you multiple of these?
- If you were a color, what color would you be? Does your color change? Are there repeating colors or other senses?
- What images or emblems keep recurring and why?
- Who are your characters or speakers?
- How do the characters or speakers grow or change?
- Do you need more or other characters?
- Are there poems where the character disappears?
- Where do the poems take place? What is the world around the poem doing?
- What season(s) do the poems take place in?
- Are there any themes or recurring themes and if so, should those themes be highlighted more or lessened?
- Are you a story and if so, is there a narrative line or arc that could be traced, even lightly?

- If there is a narrative arc, is it linear, circular, telescopic, flash-backing, questioning, violent, mosaic, spiraling, wave-like, whispering?
- Does the arc need additional meat or to be toned down?
- Can elements of fiction writing be relevant to your poems?
- Are there arguments or tensions amongst the poems and if so, how?
- Is there room for the reader to learn and grow, to make their own experience?

Repeat this process over and over until some kind of vision appears. This vision may appear in your dreams or while you take a walk or while you are talking to a fellow poet about your poems. This vision may appear in an image or through words or through song or color. For a bonsai, if I shut my eyes, I can begin to see a possible shape, what it not only wants to be, but what shape it might most comfortably take.

You could even stack poems into groupings based on these questions and those stackings may bias toward a vision. Heather Christle worked with her editor to code aspects of her manuscript that would ultimately become *The Crying Book*, a book of lyrical prose. The moon was silver, whiteness was vermilion, science was yellow, language and literature were green, autobiography was blue but depended on time (young was peri-winkle and older was azure). Christle then went on to use her child's colored pencils to fill in small boxes on graph paper that corresponded to sections of the manuscript, looking for gaps or oversaturations in pattern. The result was a beautiful piece of visual art and a window into her man-uscript's leanings and gaps.

Although I've never done this myself, you could write a mini book review of your manuscript as a critic might. That might help you begin to see patterns or shape. This act could also help determine where the man-uscript is unfinished or unrealized.

• • •

This is also when you might think about how to challenge your own thinking. In the world of bonsai, there's something called wiring, where you use copper or aluminum wiring to train and style your bonsai by wrapping wire around the branches of the tree to bend or reposition the branches to take a new shape.

For a poetry collection, it's easy to shape the poems into three sections. Three is the smallest odd prime number. It has religious or cultural significance in many cultures. It is repeated throughout the Bible as a symbol. Countless first books are organized into three sections (including my own). Each section of a three-section book serves an important role. The first can be an introduction to your poems, your voice, etc. The middle section can be a centerpiece. The final section can extend toward the future, the unknown, or it can close the book like a bookend, holding the poems together.

But you might want to rewire your poems and bend the poems into a different shape. If you decide to try this, you might need to look more closely at the poems that you do have and write into the manuscript, meaning write new poems towards a new shape.

And some books may resist sections altogether. In an email exchange, poet Dana Levin wrote: "In Charles Simic's books, there's not really a journey. The sections function as pearls on a string." Levin then explains how she organized her third book, *Sky Burial*: "When I was organizing *Sky Burial*, Louise [Glück] told me that since every poem was about death in general and the deaths of my parents and sister specifically, AND, since the poems varied widely in formal approach and tone, to organize via difference: to startle all the way, to really change up formal approach poem by poem—to not let the reader get comfortable. She also thought that the book should have no sections, so as to read as 'one long continuous cry.'" I think of these kinds of books like a ghazal, where each couplet is a different-shaped bead in a bracelet, yet all tied together via a string. The clasp is the speaker.

Regardless, shape shouldn't just be functional. Natasha Sajé says that sections, if you are deploying them, aren't just for clarity: "Dividing a book into sections is analogous to the division of an hour into quarters, a symphony into movements, a harmony into parts; such divisions should make the experience more artful, not merely more clear" (149–162). Books that are too cleanly organized can read like textbooks or essays.

You might also need to take out poems that feel weaker or don't seem to fit with the others (sometimes you might want to intentionally keep these askew poems in a manuscript to surprise the reader). Extracting poems, though, can be difficult emotionally. When you trim a bonsai, you use a putty to seal cuts and to keep the sap from bleeding. You knead the paste into a small ball, flatten between your fingers, and apply it to the bonsai wound.

You also wound your manuscript when you take out poems, particularly if they've been in a group for a long time. One way to do this is to read each poem while it is on the floor and devise a marking system such as a check-mark for poems you feel are closer to being done and a question mark for poems that may need work or might be cut out altogether. If you do decide to cut a poem, seal the wound by knowing that you can still publish that individual poem in a journal or save it for another manuscript. Cutting it from the book doesn't mean you've killed it. It still exists. You can still read it and share it. And you've learned something while writing it.

Challenging your own thinking could also mean that you might need to be held back as Barthes says: the goal of literary work (of literature as work) is to make the reader no longer a consumer, but a producer of the text (4). What is the role of the reader? How might a book leave room for the reader to shape the experience?

I liken this process to thinking about how to raise a child. How much guiding should a parent do? How much space do you leave between you and a child? Depending on the kind of parent or writer, that space could vary. Readers, like children, are smart; you don't need to hand everything to them on a platter. The human brain looks for pattern and so will your reader, even if you didn't intend it. But readers, like children, also might need to be taught how to turn the lights on just once so they can do it on their own next time.

• • •

If your book is to have sections, you might wonder how to make those sections, similar to how you might wonder how to actually shape your bonsai. In the same way each section of a bonsai tells its own story within the whole bonsai, each section of a book is its own smaller poem within the larger book. Even if you don't have sections, a book of poems may still feel like it has a beginning, middle, and end. And with the string of pearls approach, there could still be some kind of ghostly shape.

Is the current manuscript you're working on more heavily reliant on the singular poem or the entire book? Think about *The Wild Iris* by Louise Glück versus *Praise* by Robert Hass. The first is more of a unified and co-dependent collection of poems; the latter is more of a loose grouping of poems written during a period of Hass's life.

Like the many books selected randomly from my shelf, your manuscript might desire a frontispiece poem. This poem is a kind of entryway into a new world of your poems. It could be a short poem or a long poem. It could be a trumpet, announcing the other poems, or it could be a quiet knot in a trunk that your eye naturally goes to. It could be a huge entryway to a mansion or a gate hidden by ivy. These poems often loudly or quietly grapple with larger thematic concerns in a collection. But they don't have to. They can simply be a whisper, a first sacrifice.

However many sections your manuscript might have (or even without sections), the first section/part and the last section/part are important. The first section might desire a poem or poems that provide crucial information that the reader might need to know. But these poems aren't merely informational. These poems need to labor *and* be art objects within themselves. It's important not to let the labor of a poem exceed its art. You might need to actually write one of these poems while assembling the book or you can use tissues of extracted poems to make a new one. You might also consider whether your sections need titles or epigraphs or if such tags might seem to do too much relentless announcing of the poems that follow. Sometimes selecting epigraphs can help you see an organization of the book, but you may choose to abandon them later because they are too domineering.

As Mary Ruefle writes in *Madness, Rack, and Honey*: "Auden said a poem should be more interesting than anything that might be said about it. If you take the theme out of a poem and talk about that theme, there should still be some residual being left in the poem that goes on ticking, something like, why not say it, color, something that has an effect on your central nervous system. It is not what a poem says with its mouth, it's what a poem does with its eyes" (56–7).

The last section of a book could look back and reflect on all the other poems in the book in the same way a last line or last few lines of a poem are just the parachute landing—a culmination of the flight, the anticipation, the leaping off of the plane, the pulling of the cord, the opening of the parachute, the air, the birds, the wind.

The last section of a book (or even last poem) can be like a prison door and shut with a loud click. But it could evaporate too. It could also be more postmodern, like the part of a bonsai plant that hasn't grown yet. This type of book could reach towards the ghost of the future, as in an infinite finite. There's air for the leaves to grow into but when and how those leaves will grow is unknown. This type of book reaches and stretches towards that unknown.

Basically, the last section of a book does a lot of work, if readers make it that far. And you do want them to make it that far. In the era of limited attention and social media saturation, a sign of a good book is one that a reader finishes and sets aside to reread.

You might wonder what happens within sections, what happens across sections, or un-sectioned books. If you look closely at a section of bonsai, at first it may appear chaotic, disorderly. But when you look closely, off of any major branch, you'll see that there are many smaller branches that offshoot from that branch. There's order within disorder.

Each major branch or section of a bonsai is its own kind of special highway with its loops and tangles, its knots and crossovers. But each major branch infuses into a whole. The branches share characteristics with each other but are not the same. Sections of a book are like this too.

In Brigit Pegeen Kelly's book *Song*, for example, there's a bird or bird imagery in almost every poem. I imagine the birds as a blue thread that travels across a quilt of sky, hidden in each square, its presence only obvious to those who see it. But once you see it, it's impossible to see anything else but the winding thread. This book is actually organized into four sections, but I always remember the book as a book organized by birds, with no sections and a frontispiece poem, "Song."

I wonder about different parts of not only bonsai, but of trees. How each section can't see the other side. How each section mostly grows away from the other side while holding onto the tree. Each section of a book of poems functions similarly—both reaching away yet holding onto the fingers of the rest of the poems. They can't let go or they will die. The holding on could be ever so slight, but without the fingers touching, there's no book; it would just be a bag of poems. Even with the pearls, they are held together by a string, no matter how thin or invisible.

• • •

As you go deep into the tangle of a bonsai's branches, similarly, you might also wonder how to order the poems in a manuscript or within a section. There are many ways to order poems and to imagine the permutations, and again, knowing that there is no one *right* way can be freeing. Each manuscript is like a different bonsai plant. Let the poems tell you what works for them, knowing each season may be different. Each time of day may bring about a different order, the rain or wind can affect order.

Have you ever seen windswept trees near the ocean? That same tree would be upright just a hundred yards in. Know that *this* you is going to make this book. The you next year would make a different book. The you in California would make a different book than the you in New York.

If your book has sections, each section is like a mini book. Each section might need to begin and end with certain kinds of poems. Final poems in sections might link or speak to the first poems in the next sections in a progressive way, a fractured way, an opposing way, or even in an amorphous cloud-like way.

If your book is more like a string of pearls or even different colored beads, read them aloud and see how they flow and connect as they might on a common string, while each bead maintains its own identity.

Sometimes I read the first lines and final lines of my poems one after another and start arranging them on the floor. Other times, I read all the poems aloud and pull intuitively at poems and place them one after another. Other times, the book has yearned for some kind of shift or arc that resembles a book of fiction. How has the speaker in the poems changed? How does the order express that change?

Dana Levin wrote in a Twitter post: "A persistent sense that the order of poems in a book makes an argument for the book." For certain kinds of books, the order can *be* the book, make the book. For other types of books, it may not be as important.

• • •

For my latest book, *OBIT*, I was very aware of over-uniformity, yet felt that uniformity was essential to the book. I didn't think the book should be a "long continuous cry," to quote Glück (Glück as qtd by Levin), but a series of small outbursts, more parallel to my own unique grief experience. Yet those outbursts were also punctuated by moments of happiness, hope, and silent crying. I sprinkled a series of tankas about children throughout the book, as well as a centerpiece of more open elegies for life pre-children (with caesuras and no punctuation). The obituary poems were small fragments of death and grieving, which is how I experienced grief due to my parents' extended illnesses. In hindsight, these formal variations reflected the kaleidoscopic grief that I experienced.

In terms of the order of poems, I read the last and first lines of each poem and ordered the book that way. As the book progresses, things change: the speaker, the world around the speaker, and even grief changes. There's a ghost of chronology, but because grief and memory defy the time-space continuum, nothing is in chronological order.

Most recently in a new manuscript, I cut up a series of small poems and put two on each page because each poem seemed to want a counterpoint or a friend, so that the second poem on each page could be read antiphonally to the first. I used tape and taped two on each page, starting with my favorite poems first.

This process also led me to rework many of my less favored poems in the second half of the manuscript. I also had a friend read the manuscript. He highlighted his favorites which I noted. He wrote: "Maybe reconsider a few weaker ones. And if the pairings are NOT intentional, in terms of an antiphonal reading, perhaps reconsider some pairings." Then I asked him to highlight the weaker poems. I proceeded to rewrite all of those and sent the whole thing back.

I then sent the manuscript to another friend, who wrote back: "You might want to stay a bit longer with these poems, to arrange/rearrange some more within the lines. I think there are more secrets to be found, and more clarities." And I am now in the process of reworking the poems based on this feedback.

All of which is to say, rely on your people. If you don't have people, you need to find your people. Ask friends or even people you don't know well to do an exchange, helping each other by identifying problems with the manuscript's structure, order, poems, etc. You might take a workshop specifically to identify friends to exchange poems and manuscripts with. Behind each book of poems can be many people who work together to coax it towards something originally unimaginable by just one person.

• • •

Once you have something that resembles a book, you might need to keep working on it for a long time, sometimes months, sometimes years, sometimes decades. A bonsai requires continuous pruning. There are scissors, shears, branch cutters, root cutters, pliers, saws, hooks, rakes, etc.

If all else fails, you could always order the poems like Charles Wright did, which is to order them according to when you wrote them. Or you could just toss the poems down the stairs and then pick up poems randomly as you walk down and order the book that way, saying that your book was ordered by fate. But I don't recommend either unless this process is integral to the book itself.

At some point, you might need to turn your manuscript into a publisher. Or you can't find a publisher and decide to move on for the moment. Or you can't bear to read the manuscript poem by poem for the one thousandth time. That's when you let it go. You set it free.

And you move onto the next bonsai. The process of writing poems and making a book is never wasted. Making art can sometimes feel like it eludes instruction. But the instruction occurs in the individual process, in the making. Even if a book never gets published, you have learned something for the next bonsai.

My own goal is to keep the last two bonsais alive. But if I can't, I will make another bonsai. A bonsai is like a poem or a book of poems in that it is a made thing, not like a tree in a forest that is self-sufficient. And because we are poets, we make things. We use language to make things. Language is enacted by us. And it also enacts us, keeps us alive. You just have to start trying, to get on your knees and shuffle the poems around, as if praying. Because in the end, so much about poetry is about faith.

Works Cited

Barthes, Roland., et al. *S/Z* . 1st American ed., Hill and Wang, 1974.

Christle, Heather. "Approach to Piecing Together a Book," *Lithub*, November 5, 2019, https://lithub.com/on-the-patchwork-approach-to-piecing-together-a-book/.

Levin, Dana. Personal Interview. March 3, 2020.

Levin, Dana, [danalevinpoet]. "A persistent sense that the order of poems in a book make an argument for the book." *Twitter*, July 11, 2020, https://twitter.com/danalevinpoet/status/1282051965132967939.

Ruefle, Mary. *Madness, Rack, and Honey*. Wave Books, 2012.

Sajé, Natasha. "Dynamic Design: The Structure of Books of Poems." *The Iowa Review*, vol. 35, no. 2, Department of English and Graduate College, University of Iowa, 2005, pp. 149–62.

Discussion Questions

1. Given the various configurations of manuscript assembly that con-tributors suggest throughout the anthology, what are some of the strategies that resonate with you? What are some of the aesthetic, formal, and seman-tic possibilities of manuscript assembly that might help you to best realize your poetry manuscript?

2. Several contributors have emphasized the importance of having a trusted second reader to help you envision your manuscript. Diane Seuss states, "There is no greater provocation to risk than to be taken seriously...To write—not for someone—but toward someone," a someone she calls an "objective other." What feedback have you received from your reader (or readers)? How might that feedback inform the order of your manuscript?

3. Christopher Salerno recommends that poets read the catalogue copy for their favorite poetry distributor and then try to write a 300-word description of their book. Write your own description of your manuscript. What have you discovered about your manuscript through the process of summarizing it?

4. Honing one's aesthetic judgment, many contributors suggest, also entails reckoning with one's own poetic origins. Consider your first forays into poetry and what you have come to value as a poet. How does your manu-script reflect these values? How have they changed through time?

5. Cyrus Cassells speaks to the legacy of poems ("Each poem is a record of the breath and body of the poet, and each book represents one's artistic and spiritual journey"), and the pleasure of creating a visual and poetic signature of aesthetic continuity across his collections. Can you articulate what legacy you aspire your poems or manuscript to have in a reader's mind? How do the animating forces of your poems inform those of your manuscript?

6. Several contributors underscore the tension between mystery and technique, and how to balance between experiential process, and structural, organizational, and formal concerns. "Give yourself free rein to play," says Annie Finch, echoing Karyna McGlynn, whose essay describes her work with surrealist collage, as a "twin impulse" to her poetic practice. What freeing and formalist techniques might you try as you navigate the book assembly process using both intuition and logic, within language or in other mediums such as music and the visual arts?

7. Consider an essay in the anthology that resonated with you. Read a poetry collection that the author has written. What did you learn about the poet's collection vis-à-vis their procedural aesthetics, as articulated? What structuring principles seem to apply to the collection? How has your reading of poetry collections developed or changed, in light of reading this anthology?

Acknowledgments

THIS ANTHOLOGY WOULD not be possible without the ingenuity and dedication of our twelve contributors, who are the reason this book came into being: Diane Seuss, Heather Treseler, Christopher Salerno, Annie Finch, Stephen Kampa, Alyse Knorr, Harvey Hix, Karyna McGlynn, Philip Metres, Kazim Ali, Cyrus Cassells, and Victoria Chang. Grateful acknowledgment is also made to *Poets & Writers*, publisher of Diane Seuss's essay "Restless Herd: Some Thoughts on Order—In Poetry, in Life," and to *AWP Chronicle*, publisher of Annie Finch's essay "The Body of the Poetry Manuscript: Patterning Your Collection with Structural Repetition." We would also like to thank Jon Stephen Miller, Mary Biddinger, Thea Ledendecker, Amy Freels, and Brook Wyers at The University of Akron Press for adding this volume to their Series in Contemporary Poetics catalogue and for their kind, encouraging, and steadfast support throughout the editorial and production process, and for believing in this project, sparked by an Emily Dickinson quote and conceptual metaphors of drafting and completing, imagining and realizing, making and unmaking, as well as the aporias and mysticism surrounding the process of assembling a poetry manuscript: a creative impulse that can, like all good poems, be perceived aslant or intuitively, as well as theorized and made legible. "I gathered you together" (150), Louise Glück writes in her poem "September Twilight": to find readers like you.

Work Cited

Glück, Louise. *The Wild Iris*. The Ecco Press, 1992.

Contributors

Kazim Ali was born in the United Kingdom and has lived transnationally in the United States, Canada, India, France, and the Middle East. His books encompass multiple genres, including the volumes of poetry *Inquisition*; *Sky Ward*, winner of the Ohioana Book Award in Poetry; *The Far Mosque*, winner of Alice James Books' New England/New York Award; *The Fortieth Day*; *All One's Blue*; and the cross-genre texts *Bright Felon* and *Wind Instrument*. His novels include the recently published *The Secret Room: A String Quartet*, and among his books of essays are the hybrid memoir *Silver Road: Essays, Maps & Calligraphies* and *Fasting for Ramadan: Notes from a Spiritual Practice*. He is also an accomplished translator (of Marguerite Duras, Sohrab Sepehri, Ananda Devi, Mahmoud Chokrollahi, and others) and an editor of several anthologies and books of criticism. After a career in public policy and organizing, Ali taught at various colleges and universities, including Oberlin College, Davidson College, St. Mary's College of California, and Naropa University. He is currently a Professor of Literature at the University of California, San Diego. His newest books are a volume of three long poems entitled *The Voice of Sheila Chandra* and a memoir of his Canadian childhood, *Northern Light*.

Victoria Chang's latest book of poetry is *The Trees Witness Everything* (Copper Canyon Press). Her nonfiction book, *Dear Memory* (Milkweed Editions), was published in 2021. *OBIT* (Copper Canyon Press, 2020), was named a *New York Times Notable Book*, a *Time Must-Read Book*, and received the *Los Angeles Times* Book Prize, the Anisfield-Wolf Book Award in Poetry, and the PEN/Voelcker Award. It was also longlisted for a National Book Award and named a finalist for the National Book Critics Circle Award and the Griffin International Poetry Prize. She has received a Guggenheim Fellowship, lives in Los Angeles, and is a Core Faculty member within Antioch's low-residency MFA Program.

Cyrus Cassells is the 2021 Poet Laureate of Texas. His most recent book, *The World That the Shooter Left Us*, was published in 2022, and his ninth book, *Is There Room for Another Horse on Your Horse Ranch?*, a finalist for the National Poetry Series, will be published in 2024. Among his honors: a Guggenheim fellowship, the 1981 National Poetry Series, a Lambda Literary Award, a Lannan Literary Award, two NEA grants, a Pushcart Prize, and the William Carlos Williams Award. His 2018 volume, *The Gospel According to Wild Indigo*, was a finalist for the NAACP Image Award. *Still Life with Children: Selected Poems of Francesc Parcerisas*, translated from the Catalan, was awarded the Texas Institute of Letters' Soeurette Diehl Fraser Award for Best Translated Book of 2018 and 2019. His second volume of Catalan translations, *To The Cypress Again and Again: Tribute to Salvador Espriu*, will be published in 2023. He was nominated for the 2019 Pulitzer Prize in Criticism for his cultural reviews in *The Washington Spectator*. He teaches in the MFA program at Texas State University and received the 2021 Presidential Award for Scholarly/Creative Activities, one the university's highest honors.

Annie Finch is the author of six books of poetry, including *Eve* (finalist for the National Poetry Series and Yale Series of Younger Poets), *Calendars* (finalist for the National Poetry Series and Foreword Book Award), and *Spells: New and Selected Poems* (Maine Women Writers Award) as well as the epic poem *Among the Goddesses: An Epic Libretto in Seven Dreams* (Sarasvati Award). Finch's poetry has appeared in *Poetry*, *The Paris Review*, *The New York Times*, and *The Penguin Book of Twentieth-Century American Poetry* and been translated into a dozen languages including Russian and Farsi. Her other books include *The Body of Poetry: Essays on Women, Form, and the Poetic Self*, *The Ghost of Meter*, eight edited and coedited anthologies of poetics including *A Formal Feeling Comes*, *Villanelles*, and *Measure for Measure*, the poetry textbook *A Poet's Craft*, and *Choice Words*, the first major anthology of literature on abortion. She is also the translator of the complete poems of French poet Louise Labé for the University of Chicago Press. She has collaborated on opera and verse drama productions with artists in dance, music, and theater and performed her work as Poetry Witch at venues including The Cathedral of St. John the Divine, Deepak Chopra Homespace, and the Jaipur Literary Festival in India. Finch holds a B.A. from Yale and a PhD from Stanford, has taught widely, and served for a decade as Director of the Stonecoast MFA Program in Creative Writing. She has lectured at universities including Berkeley, Toronto, Harvard, and Oxford, and in 2010 she was awarded the Robert Fitzgerald Award for her lifetime contribution to the art and craft of versification. She is an Emeritus Fellow of Black Earth Institute and serves on the Advisory Board for the Association for the Study of Women and Mythology. She is the Founder and Director of PoetryWitchCommunity. org, where she teaches poetry, meter, scansion, and magic.

Sarah Giragosian is the author of the poetry collections *Queer Fish*, a winner of the American Poetry Journal Book Prize (Dream Horse Press, 2017) and *The Death Spiral* (Black Lawrence Press, 2020). Sarah's writing has appeared in such journals as *Orion*, *Ecotone*, *The Missouri Review*, *Tin House*, and *Prairie Schooner*, among others. She teaches at the University at Albany-SUNY.

H. L. Hix's recent books include a novel, *The Death of H. L. Hix*; an edition and translation of *The Gospel* that merges canonical with noncanonical sources in a single narrative, and refers to God and Jesus without assigning them gender; a poetry collection, *How It Is That We*; an edition, with Julie Kane, of selected poems by contemporary Lithuanian poet Tautvyda Marcinkevičiūtė, called *Terribly In Love*; an essay collection, *Demonstrategy*; and an anthology of "poets and poetries, talking back," *Counterclaims*. He professes philosophy and creative writing at a university in "one of those square states." His website is www.hlhix.com.

Stephen Kampa holds a BA in English Literature from Carleton College and an MFA in Poetry from the Johns Hopkins University. His first book, *Cracks in the Invisible*, won the 2010 Hollis Summers Poetry Prize and the 2011 Gold Medal in Poetry from the Florida Book Awards. His second book, *Bachelor Pad*, and his third book, *Articulate as Rain*, both appeared from The Waywiser Press. His work has also appeared in *The Best American Poetry*. Recently, he was the poet-in-residence at the Amy Clampitt House. He teaches at Flagler College.

Alyse Knorr is an associate professor of English at Regis University and co-editor of Switchback Books. She is the author of the poetry collections *Mega-City Redux* (Green Mountains Review, 2017); *Copper Mother* (Switchback Books, 2016); and *Annotated Glass* (Furniture Press Books, 2013); the nonfiction book *Super Mario Bros. 3* (Boss Fight Books, 2016); and four poetry chapbooks. Her work has appeared or is forthcoming in *The New Republic, Poetry Magazine, Alaska Quarterly Review, Denver Quarterly*, and *The Georgia Review*, among others. She received her MFA from George Mason University.

Virginia Konchan is the author of four poetry collections: *Bel Canto* (Carnegie Mellon University Press, 2022), *Hallelujah Time* (Véhicule Press, 2021), *Any God Will Do* and *The End of Spectacle* (Carnegie Mellon UP, 2020 and 2018), and a short story collection, *Anatomical Gift* (Noctuary Press, 2017). Her work has appeared in *The New Yorker, The Atlantic, The New Republic*, and *The American Poetry Review*, and she teaches at the Cleveland Institute of Art.

Karyna McGlynn is a writer, professor, and collagist. She is the author of three poetry collections from Sarabande Books: *50 Things Kate Bush Taught Me About the Multiverse* (2022), *Hothouse* (2017), and *I Have to Go Back to 1994 and Kill a Girl* (2009). Karyna holds an MFA in Poetry from the University of Michigan, a PhD in Creative Writing & Literature from the University of Houston, and a Wisconsin Institute of Creative Writing Fellowship. Recent honors include a *New York Times* Editor's Choice, the Rumi Prize for Poetry, and the *Florida Review* Editors' Award in Fiction. With Erika Jo Brown and Sasha Debevec-McKenney, she's co-editing the anthology *Clever Girl: Witty Poetry by Women*. She's also designing a collaged tarot deck called *Paper Arcana*. Karyna is Director of Creative Writing at Interlochen Center for the Arts.

Philip Metres is the author of ten books, including *Shrapnel Maps* (2020), *The Sound of Listening: Poetry as Refuge and Resistance* (2018), *Pictures at an Exhibition* (2016), *Sand Opera* (2015), *I Burned at the Feast: Selected*

Poems of Arseny Tarkovsky (2015), and others. His work has garnered the Guggenheim Fellowship, the Lannan Fellowship, two NEAs, seven Ohio Arts Council Grants, the Hunt Prize, the Adrienne Rich Award, three Arab American Book Awards, the Watson Fellowship, the Lyric Poetry Prize, Creative Workforce Fellowship, and the Cleveland Arts Prize. He is professor of English and director of the Peace, Justice, and Human Rights program at John Carroll University, and Core Faculty at Vermont College of Fine Arts. http://www.philipmetres.com.

Christopher Salerno is the author of five books of poetry. His most recent book, *The Man Grave*, won the Lexi Rudnitsky Award from Persea Books. Previous books include *Sun & Urn* (UGA Poetry Prize), ATM (Georgetown Poetry Prize), *Minimum Heroic* (Mississippi Review Poetry Prize), and *Whirligig*. His trade book, *How to Write Poetry: A Guided Journal*, is available from Calisto Media. His work has received the Glenna Luschei Award from *Prairie Schooner*, The Founders Prize from RHINO Magazine, the Two Sylvias Press Chapbook Award, the Laurel Review Chapbook Prize, and a New Jersey State Council on the Arts fellowship. His poems have appeared in *The New York Times Magazine*, *The New Republic*, *The American Poetry Review*, *New England Review*, and elsewhere. He teaches in the MFA program at William Paterson University in New Jersey, where he serves as Director of Writing Across the Curriculum.

Diane Seuss is the author of five books of poetry. Her most recent collection is *frank: sonnets* (Graywolf Press, 2021), a winner of the Pulitzer Prize, the PEN/Voelcker Prize, the Los Angeles Times Book Prize, and the National Book Critics Circle Award. *Still Life with Two Dead Peacocks and a Girl*, (Graywolf Press 2018) was a finalist for the National Book Critics Circle Award and the Los Angeles Times Book Prize. *Four-Legged Girl* (Graywolf Press, 2015) was a finalist for the Pulitzer Prize. Seuss is a 2020 Guggenheim Fellow. She received the John Updike Award from the American Academy of Arts and Letters in 2021 and was a finalist for the 2022 Kingsley Tufts Poetry Award, Claremont Graduate University. Seuss has taught in several creative writing programs, including as a visiting professor at Colorado College, the University of Michigan, and Washington University in St. Louis. She was raised by a single mother in rural Michigan, which she continues to call home.

Heather Treseler is the author of *Parturition* (2020), which won the international chapbook award from the Munster Literature Centre in Cork, Ireland, and the Jean Pedrick Chapbook Prize from the New England Poetry Club. Her poems appear in *The American Scholar*, *Cincinnati Review*, *PN Review*, and *The Iowa Review*, among other journals, and her essays appear in eight books about modernist and contemporary poetry as well as in the *Los Angeles Review of Books*, *Harvard Review*, and *Boston Review*. Her poem "Wildlife" was chosen for the W. B. Yeats Prize (2021) by Spencer Reece and her sequence of poems "The Lucie Odes" was selected for *The Missouri Review*'s Jeffrey E. Smith Editors' Prize (2019). She is a professor of English and Presidential Fellow in the Arts at Worcester State University and a resident scholar at the Women's Studies Research Center at Brandeis University. Her work has been supported by residencies at the Boston Athenæum, the T. S. Eliot House, and the American Academy of Arts and Sciences. She lives by the Charles River outside of Boston.

Sarah Giragosian is the author of the poetry collections *Queer Fish*, a winner of the American Poetry Journal Book Prize (Dream Horse Press, 2017) and *The Death Spiral* (Black Lawrence Press, 2020). Sarah's writing has appeared in such journals as *Orion*, *Ecotone*, *The Missouri Review*, *Tin House*, and *Prairie Schooner*, among others. She teaches at the University at Albany-SUNY.

Virginia Konchan is the author of four poetry collections: *Bel Canto* (Carnegie Mellon University Press, 2022), *Hallelujah Time* (Véhicule Press, 2021), *Any God Will Do* and *The End of Spectacle* (Carnegie Mellon UP, 2020 and 2018), and a short story collection, *Anatomical Gift* (Noctuary Press, 2017). Her work has appeared in *The New Yorker*, *The Atlantic*, *The New Republic*, and *The American Poetry Review*, and she teaches at the Cleveland Institute of Art.

Printed in the United States
by Baker & Taylor Publisher Services